THE WHIRLING DERVISH

RUMI DEMYSTIFIED

Avi Raa

The Whirling Dervish

ACKNOWLEDGEMENT

The whole universe has to come together to move a single blade of grass. This book would not have been possible without the support of everything that has ever happened. I am especially grateful to my students, who record, transcribe, edit, and publish my talks.

The Whirling Dervish

TABLE OF CONTENTS

The Whirling Dervish

INTRODUCTION

Rumi was a 13th century Sufi mystic, one of the most beloved and influential poets of all time. His poetry is known for its beauty, depth, and wisdom. It explores a wide range of spiritual themes, including love, longing, union with the divine, and the nature of reality.

Rumi's poetry is a celebration of love in all its forms. He writes about the passionate love between lovers, the mystical love between the soul and the divine, and the universal love that connects all beings. His poetry is also infused with a sense of longing. He writes about the soul's longing for union with the divine, the lover's longing for the beloved, and the human being's longing for meaning and purpose.

In "The Whirling Dervish," Avi offers a unique and insightful perspective on the work of Rumi. He takes us on a magical journey through the labyrinth of our inner selves, revealing the treasures of wisdom hidden in Rumi's enchanting poetry.

Avi's interpretation of Rumi's poetic verses is both contemporary and illuminating. He introduces us to a Rumi that we have always longed to connect with - a mystic drunk in love, expounding some of the deepest secrets of life using delicate, artfully chosen words.

The book explores Rumi's use of metaphors and imagery to describe the mystical experience of love. Avi draws on his own personal experiences and insights to offer a fresh and accessible interpretation of Rumi's work, exploring themes of individuality, self-expression, and a vision of a world in which all beings are united in the drunken ecstasy of love.

Throughout the book, Avi emphasizes the relevance of Rumi's teachings for our lives today. He shows how Rumi's insights can help us to navigate the challenges of modern life and to find our way to a more meaningful and fulfilling existence.

Avi's book is an invaluable resource for anyone who is longing to explore the unfathomable depths of Rumi's poetry and teachings. It is also a guide-book on the mystical path of love for anyone who is searching for inspiration on their own spiritual journey.

THE LANGUAGE OF LOVE

Of all the different ways of searching, love is the highest. This is because it is only in love that the searcher disappears. When the searcher disappears, arriving happens. This is what makes a spiritual quest different from every other thing we search for in life. All other things we search for, we are searching to experience or to possess. Only in spirituality are we searching to become.

Love is the highest form of searching because when there is love, when a moment is filled with love, it can accommodate nothing else. Love is so complete, so expansive, so deep, that all the ideas of you, me, searching, desiring, awakening, and enlightenment simply drop away. When you are experiencing love, love itself is the experiencer. Love itself is the one that is experiencing, and love is the experience.

There is no way to describe such a search. There are no methods or techniques. The path of love is unique and cannot be compared to any other method of searching. This is because the moment you remove the journey and replace it with longing, the way you long is unique. It is your own way of longing. You cannot learn from someone else's longing. You cannot learn from someone else's love.

The path of love is unlike many other meditation techniques or methods through which you can reach awakening. With other methods, you can learn from the experiences of others. You can ask for the method and try to replicate it inside of you because what is being passed on is pure knowledge and wisdom. The depth and intensity can be supplied.

Once you understand the method and the approach, you will also understand that you have to approach this technique with a deeper desire to understand it. However, there is no difficulty understanding the method. You sit quietly, close your eyes, watch your breath, and don't drift off into thoughts or fall asleep. Stay awake and aware, and be as close to your body as possible. This is language that is easy to understand and familiar.

However, searching through love cannot accommodate any of this. To the one who is drunk in love, this language does not even make sense because they do not see that what they are searching for has something to do with the outside world. They do not see that it is something that is outside of them.

When you are searching for the truth through love, you know that you have to become it. You know that you are the obstacle. Your mind is the obstacle. Your body is the obstacle. Therefore, the language of love is very different from the language of the world. It is the language of love that gives rise to poetry. When you are drunk, you cannot speak straight. You cannot make too much sense. You cannot be too logical or structured. You sing. You cry. You express yourself. You dance. You move.

When words lose all their civility, when they do not want to respect anyone, when they do not want to conform to any accepted beliefs, they become poetry. Poetry is words dancing in absolute freedom. Words have their own meaning in poetry, and the meaning is how you understand it. The very same words can be read in two completely different ways by two people. This is because it is like watching someone dance, watching someone sing, or watching someone in a moment of deep ecstasy and joy. Depending on your level of depth and understanding, you see it in your own way.

This is why no two individuals can ever read the same poem in the same way. Give them the same words, and they will still be thrown into two different spaces of imagination. If poetry is the dance of words, then love is its ornamentation. Nothing embellishes poetry like love. Nothing makes words dance like love. In fact, when there is no love, poetry is dull and dry, and easily understandable. When there is no love, it is the mind speaking. The language of the mind is easy to understand because the mind did not create the language. It simply borrowed it from here and there. So, when someone is speaking purely through their mind, it is not hard to understand them. And they are not talking about anything profound or deep.

However, when you are reading or listening to something, and it is stirring something inside of you, it is drawing you into that dance. But the whole experience is covered in mystery. You do not know exactly what it is that you are listening to. The most profound poetry is always mysterious. You understand something, but you know that there is a lot more that remains to be understood.

In the world of poetry and in the world of love, there have been beautiful expressions of the human heart expressing its longing. For example, the Indian poet Rabindranath Tagore's Gitanjali is a collection of songs that he composed as a longing to connect to something beyond his understanding. It took a long time for us to recognize the profundity of these words. The sheer volume of his poetry was also a factor. It took decades for someone to finish reading all of his poetry before recognizing its immensity and awarding him the Nobel Prize.

Tagore was not creating his poetry for any purpose. He was simply singing these songs. And when you sing, when you are longing for something, you will continue to sing until the union happens. There is no question of "I have covered everything. I have expressed myself in as many ways as I can." In fact, Tagore said at the end of his life, after composing one of the longest and most comprehensive sets of his poetic verses, "I could not present my offering to the divine the way I wanted to. I have failed. I have tried, but I have failed. My songs are not complete. I still want to sing them. My heart is still empty." In fact, he says, "I have said so much, but I have actually not said anything."

Only a lover can understand the meaning of these words. For a lover, until the union happens, whatever you have done longing for that union is useless. It is only that union that completes and adds meaning to that longing. Tagore was deep and mystical, but he was not enlightened or awakened. So when you read Gitanjali, you read it with a lot of pain in your heart. It is impossible not to read Gitanjali and feel a sense of helplessness, a sense of awe and wonder for something that you cannot see, something that you cannot understand. That feeling of how inadequate the mind is, how inadequate the body is to long for something as grand as the divine.

Rumi falls into a completely different category. Of all the different poets, Rumi stands alone because he was enlightened. He was awakened. His songs are unique in that they express both longing and union. Rumi's poems cannot be understood in the traditional sense. You cannot understand the state of his mind by reading them. There is no structure to his poems. They are as random as a thought crossing your mind, and he does not even try to go beyond that randomness. He expresses himself just the way he is experiencing something inside. He moves from one idea to another without any care for trying to connect those two ideas.

Rumi is so deep in the experience of love, so rooted in his being that there is no necessity for him to hold on to one particular idea for any longer than he needs to. He can move from one idea to another because he sees the same love, the same longing, and the same union in everything, everywhere.

There is no restriction in terms of what he can use to communicate that longing. The only way to understand Rumi is to understand longing, to understand humanity's ultimate search, and to understand a state of no mind and no body. You have to start somewhere, and if you have not yet reached that state of transcendence, you have to look for it in his poetry. You have to feel it. You have to experience it.

Rumi was a Persian poet. He met an individual named Shams of Tabrizi, a wandering mystic. Up until then, Rumi was just another seeker. He did not even know that he was searching. Like many people, they go about their lives knowing that they are searching for something, but they do not know what it is. It was Shams of Tabrizi, an enlightened mystic himself, who reignited Rumi's quest for self-realization. With Shams' help, Rumi became enlightened. As a dedication to him, Rumi sang these songs.

Rumi's poetry is unique in multiple dimensions. First, it is a poetry dedicated to his friend. He keeps coming back to the same theme: "This is to my friend, Shams of Tabrizi." But the depth of longing is beyond friendship. He is in a state of intoxication. You can feel this in every verse. This is not a sober man sitting on a chair, writing his poetry in a book sitting on a desk. When you read Rumi, it feels like he has drunk too much, been thrown out of the tavern, and has staggered to the curb. He is sitting on the curb, composing this poetry.

You get the feeling that this is a man who does not care where he is, how he looks, or what people think of him. He seems to be everywhere. There are moments when he is in the middle of the bustling movement of human civilization, watching everything that man has created. There are moments when he is in nature, and then there are moments when he is absolutely alone, within his mind and his thoughts. There are also moments when he is talking about human civilization and its structure.

Rumi is difficult to understand because it is hard to put him in any categories. Usually, poets pick a certain domain that they are interested in and express that interest in different ways. However, what Rumi talks about is so universal and transcendental that it applies to every situation he is in. Although Rumi was deeply influenced by Sufism, the mystical branch of Islam, his poetry is universal. It resonates in every part of the human longing. It goes beyond religion, politics, and the immediate reverberations of his community. Somewhere, because the longing is so deep, it transcends all social constructs to speak to you directly.

That is why his poetry is pure delight for the one who is on the path, pure delight for the one who is searching for the ultimate, but also pure anguish. For Rumi, there is no separation between him and what he is seeking. But for the one who has not yet reached the ultimate, there is that separation. However, even in that anguish, you can find comfort in the fact that what you are searching for is not far away. It is very close.

Rumi himself explains in his beautiful phrases what love is, what longing is, what the search of man is, and why your life is incomplete without love. And not just love that you want to experience and express, but the love that you want to become.

Why should I seek? I am the same as he.
His essence speaks through me.
I have been longing for myself.
Try and be a sheet of paper
with nothing on it.
Be a spot of ground where nothing is growing.
Where something might be planted,
a seed possibly from the absolute.

There is nothing to seek. The whole idea of searching is human. Existence doesn't search. 'Search' is a very shallow word. It has no depth to it. That is why existence does not care for the word search. It is only man who searches. Existence longs. There is a big difference between searching and longing. Searching is the domain of the mind. Longing belongs to the heart.

The Whirling Dervish

SING YOUR OWN SONG

God picks up the reed-flute world, and blows.
Each note is a need coming through one of us,
a passion, a longing pain.

Remember the lips
where the wind-breath originated,
and let your note be clear.
Don't try to end it.
Be your note.
I'll show you how it's enough.

Go up on the roof at night
in this city of the soul.

Let everyone climb on their roofs
and sing their notes!

Sing loud!

You are meant to be you. There is no doubt about the fact that you were created to be yourself. You're not a replica of someone else. You're not modeled on certain fixed ideas, and you were not created for a specific purpose. You were created as a possibility - as emptiness, with just the most basic ingredients necessary for you to sing your song: a flute, your lips, and the wind. Nothing more. Your mind, body, and aliveness. Nothing more. Everything outside of that is your entertainment, your audience, your extended playground.

As an individual, one of the hardest things to be aware of is how unique you are when compared to all other things in existence, when compared to everybody around you. The reason it's hard to recognize this uniqueness is due to the great effort that has gone into making you believe that you're not unique. That you don't have your own song to sing. That you don't carry anything meaningful to share. That you need to be molded, cast, and made useful, because someone, somewhere, has made it a habit to see you as something you're not meant to be - to see you as just a body, just another creature of existence, just another life.

Uniqueness is useless for the world. What will society do with a unique you? It is looking for workers; it is searching for those who can fit in. It has already created the wheel, the cog, and the spokes. Only a few spokes are missing here and there, and it wants you to fill those gaps. It does not want you to question the nature of the wheel. It does not want you to question where it's headed or its purpose, because there isn't any. The wheel was created in a state of slumber, and many lives were crushed beneath its weight. It is a wheel that carries many stains and much pain, bearing the memories of countless dreams trampled underfoot. Numerous individual lives are smothered in the name of conformity. It is largely a religious wheel - blind, dogmatic, and pointless. It cannot perceive individuality; it cannot acknowledge individuality.

For the first time in the history of humanity, you are born into a time where you can actually recognize all the forces that have attempted to suppress individuality. You can step away from all of that. You have a unique place for yourself, a distinctive space from which you can observe all that has occurred before you. You can see how only occasionally does a new flower with new fragrance and new colors bloom, while the rest remain the same. They emerge from the machinery of humans, from the factories of human society. This is why you don't find individuals; you only encounter different belief systems.

When you meet people, you're more often than not meeting a group. Very rarely do you meet an individual. When you encounter an individual, you will know immediately. That encounter will be unforgettable because you are in the presence of something so fresh and so unique that it reminds you of your own uniqueness. It reminds you of what you can be.

We are living in a world where such encounters are so rare that we have almost accepted life to be just a series of movements - a mechanical progression from yesterday to tomorrow. There isn't much singing going on there, and dancing occurs only occasionally. And even then, it has to be consciously chosen; otherwise, you forget even that. You're so occupied with being a cog in society's wheel that you forget you have your own independent melody. You are meant to sing your own song. You're not meant to merely replicate someone else's notes. That's what Rumi says: **"God picks up the reed-flute world and blows."**

What is the world? It is just entertainment. It is excitement and expression. Work, purpose, responsibility, your duties to God, to religion, and to the country are all man-made. When existence created you, it did so with no conditions. It did not create you and say, "I created you for just this purpose, and be only that." That's what man does. When man does anything in your favor, he asks for something in return. There's always an underlying contract to human relationships. This contract exists within all relationships - father and son, husband and wife, mother and daughter. There is an invisible contract. That is what defines a human relationship, because by its very nature, a contract means you are bound to it. So right from the beginning, you are born into a world of chains. Wherever you go, your interactions with people also tie you to them. And you're constantly being reminded of that.

Why is it that you have not recognized your own tune? Why does it take so much for an individual to simply be themselves? Why does it take so much to accept yourself just the way you are? Why is so much time and precious energy wasted on trying to be like someone else, trying to fit in? It's because right from the beginning, you've been told that your life is contractual - it is not free. It starts at home and then extends to your community. Your country says the same thing: "Yes, you can do whatever you want, but it's a contract. You've got to follow these rules in return for all the comforts we are providing you." It is the very nature of human societies. Is it fair? Is it unfair? It's the individual who has to ask that question. For society, it's fair. For the mind and body, it's fair. They are receiving something in return. They're sacrificing a bit of their freedom for a bit of security, a bit of help from the outside. For the mind and body, it's fine. But for the one who resides within you, the one born utterly free, the one who knows no contracts, it is unfair. It's unjust because he cannot truly be himself.

When Rumi uses the words 'God' and 'Divine', he is referring to Existence herself. God is a word that has been thoroughly misused, misunderstood, and entangled in too many things. It sounds very masculine, implying that there's someone sitting up there creating. No. That's not what Rumi means. When he says, "God picks up the reed flute world and blows," Rumi isn't saying that God created you in his image. He's not saying that God created you to be fruitful and multiply. He's not referring to the biblical God, an extension of man's ego. That is why the biblical God is purposeful - why he gives commandments. Rumi's God picks up a reed flute and blows. Rumi's God is a singing, dancing God. To Rumi, existence is merely an expression of joy, and you were born as an expression of joy.

You were conceived as a seed amidst two individuals who were at the peak of their joy. Their entire lives could have been messy; they could have been suffering and worrying constantly, living in a stressful environment. But notice the conditions that gave birth to you. They couldn't have been in pain; they couldn't have been suffering and given birth to you. At least momentarily, they had to forget all of that. They had to momentarily forget their own bodies and minds. They had to transcend to a different realm called orgasm to sow the seed called you. So you don't belong to them; you don't belong to their troubles or ideologies. They had to shed everything themselves to create the necessary conditions to give birth to you. Only when you erase the mind and body through some process - we call it sex, orgasm, or that moment when you've forgotten the mind and body and you are completely erased - are we capable of giving birth. That's where humans come from. We come from nothingness; we come from emptiness. Yes, we pick up reflections of our parents, we pick up some of their traits. We might even resemble them a bit. But we don't belong to them. Each of us is unique.

You are your own song because you were created as an expression of joy. You were born in a moment of pure ecstasy. How can there be any purpose to it? How can there be any contract there? And how can there be any comparison between you and someone else?

When you are singing, enjoy it; no two notes copy each other. They're unique.

God picks up the reed-flute world, and blows.
Each note is a need coming through one of us,
a passion, a longing pain.

Remember the lips
where the wind-breath originated,
and let your note be clear.
Don't try to end it.

Be your note.
I'll show you how it's enough.

You are complete by yourself. This is another common message of all awakened beings. Once they have discovered something within them, they have never returned from that space and said, "This is spectacular. This is wonderful. This is amazing, but you just need one other thing." All of them have said that you don't need anything else. You are complete. It is that completeness they realized within themselves, and that is why it is the highest, grandest experience they can have. Because once you've experienced completeness, by the very definition of the word, there's nothing missing in you.

As of now, you're running, chasing, and searching because something is missing. That is the mind. The mind is an unresolved desire. It's a collection of unresolved desires. When your desires are resolved, what is the necessity for the mind? What is the necessity for thinking? More importantly, what is the necessity to cling to them? Your thoughts can be in the background somewhere. You can listen to them once in a while. Because occasionally, they tell you something useful - like "you have a cold, take this tablet." Except for those occasions, your mind is just pure noise. It is useful on certain occasions, perhaps a few times a day, But we have given too much control to the mind.

Rumi is asking you to remember the source where you come from.

Go up on the roof at night
in this city of the soul.

Let everyone climb on their roofs
and sing their notes!

Sing loud!

What a transcendental change it is to look at life as a song, to look at life as a play, to look at life as a moment-to-moment experience when compared to seeing it as purposeful, fixed, goal-oriented, mechanical drag. It's easy to fall into the rabbit hole of fixed ideas. And once you fall into one of those ideas, you forget your true nature.

How is it that so many human beings, billions of them, are born as unique expressions of life, who are born with singing and dancing in their hearts, who are born full of love, full of light, can live as if life has no meaning? As if life has no purpose? How can they live as if life is a mechanical movement from the past to the future? It's because it's so easy to fall into fixed ideas, into rigid beliefs. And one fixed idea is enough to lead you away from your true nature.

THE DREAM

This place is a dream.
Only a sleeper considers it real.

Then death comes like dawn,
and you wake up laughing
at what you thought was your grief.

But there's a difference with this dream.
Everything cruel and unconscious
done in the illusion of the present world,
all that does not fade away at the death-waking.

It stays,
and it must be interpreted.

All the mean laughing,
all the quick, sexual wanting,
those torn coats of Joseph,
they change into powerful wolves
that you must face.

The retaliation that sometimes comes now,
the swift, payback hit,
is just a boy's game
to what the other will be.

You know about circumcision here.
It's full castration there!

Here, Rumi is talking about something very deep.
He's saying death is not the end of your experiences.
In fact, he coined a new word to describe this -
"death-waking." What is death-waking? Either you're
dead or you're awake. Because he knows death is not
the end, the one who has seen inside knows that
death is just an idea. You carry forward things to your
next life - you carry forward many things. That is
what he's referring to.

This world is a dream. Nothing here is real. But you
live as if it is real. You live as if you are going to be
here forever. Death will come. It will come very
swiftly to carry away everything, to take away all your
fixed ideas about life. But at the same time, what you
have done in this life carries forward.

There is something very important to understand
here. While the language Rumi is using sounds
religious, it sounds like he is talking about your
actions being judged when he says, "You know
circumcision here, but it's full castration there." It
seems like he is talking about heaven and hell, that he
is talking about the ultimate judgment where all your
actions would be weighed and then it would be
decided whether you should go to heaven or hell. But

that is not what Rumi is referring to. He is only using that language, which is familiar. And Rumi is drunk. Sometimes he speaks like a religious man. Sometimes he speaks like a poet. Sometimes he is just crying like a child.

But if you understand Rumi, if you understand the drunken state he is speaking from, you will reinterpret these words in a totally different way - not in a religious way. What he is saying is that there is a part of us that extends beyond death. The way we have lived, not our actions, not our rights and wrongs, but our level of awareness. How attached you are to your ideas or how detached you are from them. How entangled you are in the web of life or how free you are from it. This is what determines the quality of your next life.

There is a cup, and there is something inside the cup. Religions have focused only on the contents of the cup. When they talk about judgment, when they talk about your actions being judged somewhere, they are referring to the contents of the cup. They are telling you to accumulate good deeds, to accumulate merit, to leave out bad things, to stay away from sex, to stay away from all the pleasures of life, to live a good life. So it is all about the content. But Rumi is not talking about the contents of the cup, he is talking about the cup itself.

While a cup has no say in how much it wants to be attached to what is added to it, a human being has a choice. That is what separates us. We can be that cup. We can accept whatever is added to the cup without questioning or rejecting it, but we have complete choice in deciding how much we want to be attached to the contents of the cup. And that is what determines the shape of our next cup.

What is life? What is the next life? What is rebirth? We are really talking about what kind of cup you will be - which is basically form. Because what is inside is already there: your thoughts, your desires, the way you look at things, the meditativeness you have developed, the silence you have touched. It has all become a part of you. All that has become a part of you, that has seeped into your being, continues. But the shape of your cup may change depending on how attached you are to the contents.

If you are really attached, if you see yourself as a very restricted being, fully immersed in your thoughts, then you do not need a big cup. You do not need too much space. You can take birth in a very restricted, very tiny, limiting body. But imagine if you had put some distance between you and the contents of the cup. Imagine if you had put some distance between you and your thoughts. Basically, the contents of the cup are your thoughts and your physical body is the cup.

You can put a distance between not only your mind and your body, but you can also put a distance between your true self and your body. This cup of body is multilayered - it is the physical body as well as the true being.

Now imagine if you had put more space. It is inevitable that in your next life, you would need a bigger space. Yes, you would still have thoughts, but you would not be born into a world where you are tormented by thoughts. You are given more space. And if you were to ask me, "What is the difference between heaven and hell?" Hell is a very constricting place. Hell is too many people, not enough space to move around, very suffocating. Tight walls, tight doors, no good ventilation. That's what hell is. What is heaven? Openness. The more open the place, the more you can move around. It does not matter where you are, whether in heaven or hell, you will feel free.

If you were to ask for one thing, if you were going to be sent to hell - I'm pretty sure all of us are going to hell by the definition of religions - the first thing we will ask is, "Just give me a separate room. If possible, give me a backyard to walk in. I just want a little more space. There's too much burning, too much heat. Too much noise, too many people."

And think about it, your mind can create these conditions within you. And that is what Rumi is referring to. He's talking about the way you arrange your life inside - the way you understand your life matters.

That is what religions have totally misunderstood. They have taken this simple spiritual idea: that what you do in this life is important, but it's not what you do exactly. It is not the activity itself, but the way you do it. It is the way you bring yourself to those activities.

Did you live your life as if it was a task that needs to be completed? If that was your way of looking at life, if you lived every moment to accomplish things, then that is what continues. In the next life, you will be given a lot of tasks. If you had ten tasks here, in your next life, you will have a hundred. That is what he is talking about. "If you know circumcision here, it is full castration there."

In the transition from this life to the next, there is no consciousness or awareness. Therefore, things are exaggerated. So, if you have a little bit of fear in your mind in this life, the fears will multiply. This is because in this life, you can consciously intervene and control your fears. However, during the transition period, you are not aware and are completely lost in a dream space. Therefore, everything gets exaggerated.

What you do matters not in terms of the activity itself, but in terms of how you look at life. This is something more fundamental than what religions have been talking about. It is something more basic, like whether you sing more, laugh more, enjoy life more, are more in tune with the forces of life and nature, or are living in a world of your own.

Existence is heaven. Mind is hell. Are you living in existence or are you living in the mind? You create the conditions for heaven and hell right here. There is no other place. Heaven and hell are not "out there." They are the conditions that we create for ourselves. It is the way we interact with life.

Religions have misunderstood this inner-dimensional thing that is happening. They have used words and ideas to literalize the concepts of heaven and hell. These are not fixed ideas or physical things - they are just qualities. And you, as an individual, can choose. It is not in what you choose, but in how you choose to interact with what you have been given to interact with. Each individual is born into unique situations and circumstances, depending on their social background, religious background, and economic background. You are born into certain restrictions.

More often than not, you don't have a say in the contents of the cup. They are already added to you. By the time you realize that you are a cup, and that you are holding these things, it is already too late. Trying to empty your cup of all the contents is futile and pointless.

In the spiritual realm, emptying the cup happens very differently. It happens by expanding the cup - to a point where it does not even matter what the contents are. You don't try to throw out your anger. You don't try to throw out your past traumas. You don't try to throw out the negative influences of your parents, friends, family, or society. That's too much work. You don't psychoanalyze your dreams. You don't waste your time there. You just work on the cup. You expand it to a point where you have so much space that once in a while, you come to the corner, where all that is being added to you simply falls out.

Look at life. Play with it. But when it begins to disturb you, walk away. That's what meditation does. It gives you so much space that the content becomes immaterial. Your background, where you've come from, and the circumstances that shape your life are all immaterial because now you have become something more. And in that completeness, in that expansion, there is freedom. You can carry that forward to your next life. You can carry that space forward. You can carry that openness forward. The best thing, however, is not to carry anything forward; it's to awaken to your true nature so completely that there's no necessity to come back. There's no necessity to be trapped in another body. But for whatever reason, if you are unable to liberate yourself fully, at least the conditions you've created will help you find that final release in your future lives.

This groggy time we live,
this is what it's like:

A man goes to sleep in the town
where he has always lived, and he dreams he's living
in another town.

In the dream, he doesn't remember
the town he's sleeping in his bed in. He believes
the reality of the dream town.

The world is that kind of sleep.

We have forgotten that we are asleep. What a beautiful way of saying, "You were unconscious. You were asleep. Somebody took you and put you in a totally different town, a totally different environment. That is what birth is." You wake up to this strange reality, and you start exploring it, start understanding it, but you completely forget that you are asleep. You don't belong here. This is a dream world. Sooner or later, you have to wake up.

The dust of many crumbled cities
settles over us like a forgetful doze,
but we are older than those cities.

We began as a mineral. We emerged into plant life
and into the animal state, and then into being human,

And always we have forgotten our former states,
except in early spring, when we slightly recall
being green again.

That's how a person turns
toward a teacher. That's how a baby leans
toward the breast, without knowing the secret
of its desire, yet turning instinctively.

Humankind is being led along an evolving course,
through this migration of intelligences,
and though we seem to be sleeping,
there is an inner wakefulness
that directs the dream,

and that will eventually startle us back
to the truth of who we are.

We are asleep. We have forgotten that we are in a dream. However, there is something that is awake within us. If you look at the movement of the human race, if you observe the movement of existence, you can see that an invisible force, which is aware of the awakened nature of all creatures, is pushing them towards awakening. Every moment, an individual becomes a little more intelligent, a little more aware of their surroundings, and a little more capable of moving around. It is not their choice. It is existence that is reminding them of their true nature.

Something very significant is being conveyed. It is saying that sooner or later, you will be startled awake, because something inside you is aware that you are asleep and you need to be awakened. That is how you instinctively turn to the teacher. That is how a baby instinctively finds its mother's breasts. So many things happen without instructions in existence. They are all instinctively moving towards something. They all instinctively understand something. How is this happening?

There's great intelligence at the heart of things. However, the only problem is that because existence is so vast, there are so many creatures and so many different ways of falling asleep, it takes a really long time for existence to fully awaken all its creatures - lifetime after lifetime after lifetime. That's why it could not awaken you when you were a mineral. It tried to awaken you and created a plant out of you. It tried to awaken you again as a plant and created an animal out of you. When it tried to awaken you from your animal nature, it created a human being. Now, it's trying to awaken you through the limitations of being human, and what that awakening will be, no one knows. What the next progression after a human being is, no one knows. It can go on for a very long time - it has already taken such a long time for human beings to evolve from minerals to this point.

But the inner stirring to awaken remains the same. The desire is the same. However, because we are so attached to the dream, if existence doesn't perfectly focus on you and you alone, you'll fall back to sleep. Even if it forgets you for a single moment, you go back to sleep, and it has to come back and start again. This is what unconsciousness is. This is why it has taken so long. This is also why you cannot simply leave your awakening to existence. Yes, it will awaken you someday, maybe after another ten thousand years, after you've exhausted all your dreaming, desiring, chasing, and running. When you are exhausted and have nothing else to do, you will awaken. But you have to go through all of that.

There is another simpler way - the conscious way. You can choose to awaken yourself. You cannot awaken the human race. You cannot awaken all the species of existence; they are asleep. Existence is trying to awaken them in its own way, slowly. However, as an individual, you can take the highway to awakening. You can move away from the crowded streets and create your own path where there are no obstacles.

On the path of existence, there are a lot of obstacles because there are so many other creatures to awaken. Existence looks at everything in totality; it does not identify one individual and try to create unique conditions for that individual to awaken. It tries to awaken the whole of existence at a subconscious level by adding more intelligence and awareness to it. This realization occurs in every generation; we are becoming more intelligent and aware, yet we are still asleep. However, there are examples of individuals who have awakened even when the human race was not as intelligent or aware as it is now. They have woken up by their own choice while everybody around them was asleep.

That seeking, that searching - that's where your uniqueness comes into the picture. You're not meant to be just another cog in the wheel; you are meant to awaken yourself. This uniqueness gives you the possibility to awaken in your own unique way, disregarding the laws and rules of society and even, to a certain extent, existence. Individuals can break even the fixed laws of existence; that's how free we are. When existence created us, it did so perfectly and uniquely, not even binding us to the basic laws of existence like birth and death. An individual can choose to transcend even death. This is how spectacular the phenomenon of individuality is. Realizing this is walking the path.

DRUNK IN LOVE

Advice doesn't help lovers!
They're not the kind of mountain stream
you can build a dam across.

An intellectual doesn't know
what the drunk is feeling!

Don't try to figure
what those lost inside love
will do next!

Someone in charge would give up all his power,
if he caught one whiff of the wine musk
from the room where the lovers are doing who-knows-
what!

One of them tries to dig a hole through a mountain.
One flees from academic honors.
One laughs at famous mustaches!

There is the world of the intellectual, and then there
is the world of the drunk - two worlds separated by a
great immensity. Both are experiencing life at a certain
level in the same way. They're walking, they're talking,
they're dreaming. Sometimes they are dancing.

Sometimes they're writhing in pain. From the outside, it's the same world and the same experiences. The one who's truly drunk, who's fully intoxicated but hasn't lost his sense of balance, hasn't lost his consciousness - that is the drunk Rumi is talking about; the one who's drunk in love, the one who's drunk in the divine, in the purity of his own being. He lives in the same world as the intellectual. He goes about life the same way.

But there is a great difference separating both of their experiences. One is lost. He's searching for himself in everything. The other is filled with himself. Try to entice a man who is drunk, who's fully intoxicated, by offering him all that the world can offer - the things an intellectual is chasing. He would not care for even the greatest desires of the mind. The intellectual is simply the one who is searching in the realm of his mind. He's chasing after images. That is what he calls his dreams - "I want to accomplish my dreams." Without knowing that it is a dream, how can you accomplish a dream? How can you see the same dream again? You're dreaming about something. Can't you realize that by the time you get there, you would be in a new dream? By the very nature of dreaming, you are always moving from one dream to another. And yet, you believe that one of these dreams can actually become a reality. Existentially, it is impossible, but in your mind, you believe that it's possible.

That is what you call your life. The one who's drunk, the one who's intoxicated in love, in truth, in being, doesn't care about turning his dreams into reality. He laughs at his dreams. He sees the futility of his dreams. He plays with them once in a while and he even chases them occasionally. But his chasing is very different from your chasing. His chasing is like a child chasing a butterfly. There is no purpose. He does not even know what he's going to do if he catches the butterfly. For all you know, he's going to let it go again. He's just playing with his thoughts, playing with his dreams. He's playing with life.

On the other hand, an intellectual is serious. He's making plans on how to catch that butterfly. He's creating a strategy and approach. He doesn't even know what he will do when he catches the butterfly. But because he sees many chasing their own imaginary butterflies, he thinks that is his purpose. For the one who is unfamiliar with the deeper realms of himself, images appear to be intoxicating by themselves. He has not tasted anything deeper, so just the difference between one image and another is enough for him to start chasing.

A man who has lived in the world of imagination, in the world of his dreams, values one dream over another because that is the game he is playing. He's flipping through different images, and once in a while, if something catches his attention, he wants to experience that image in all its dimensions. It is really an image that he sees in his mind, but he's not satisfied with just the image because he can only see the image - he cannot touch it, taste it, or walk around it. So, he wants to bring all his senses to experience that image in as many different ways as he can. That is what he calls dreaming and chasing those dreams.

That is the occupation of Man. Almost his entire addiction is to images. He doesn't even know that. He thinks he's actually moving towards something real, that he's moving towards a real experience. But in reality, he's only trying to make a dream more real. He's thinking that if he can experience this dream more clearly, if he's able to navigate inside his dream, if he can be there for as long as he wants, it will become a reality. That is why he's always out there somewhere chasing things. Because there are so many images, he wants to be in some of those images - the reality he is in now is not an image. It is not changing. It is not flashing or shifting. It is too dull, too boring.

He can be living the best life possible. He can have fresh air to breathe, food to eat, and a comfortable place to rest. He can have a few books to read. He can have a cup of coffee to drink. He can have a little bit of space to walk. A nice bed to sleep in. For the one who knows what life is, these are luxuries. These are great comforts. But for the one who is chasing and cannot be in the present moment, he does not even recognize any of this. His life is incomplete. Something is missing. When he sleeps, all he can think about is what he's going to do when he wakes up. When he wakes up, all he can think about is how he can chase the dreams of his sleep. So he's never experiencing life. He's only thinking about it. And what is he trying to do? He's trying to take a simple two-dimensional image and turn that into a three-dimensional image so that his whole body can be placed into that experience - so that he can experience that two-dimensional image in all its depth. That is how simple the life of an intellectual is. That is how pointless, mindless chasing is. And yet, that is the reality of the human race.

Rumi says, "You cannot convince a lover with this intellectual game. You cannot create a barrier for the one who knows how to love." And Rumi's love is not human love. We have desecrated the word 'love' to such an ordinary level that we use it for all things that have nothing to do with love - "I love this." "I love that." We use the word as if it has no real meaning. We almost use it as a substitute for 'like.' "I love my new shoes." How? Tell me. Tell me, how do you love your shoes? What do you do with them? It's beyond my imagination. At most, you can admire your shoes.

You can be thankful for your shoes, or you can like your shoes. What is this? "I love my shoes." How deep is that connection? Do you sleep with your shoes? Otherwise, why use the word 'love'? But that is the tragedy of the word 'love.' It has been abused by overusing it. That is not the love Rumi is talking about. He's talking about love as purity, as something that a human being has to long for within themselves - something that is already inside a human being. They're busy chasing. They're busy running after butterflies. So they're not in touch with love.

Love for a mystic like Rumi is the ultimate destination. Love is what you are searching for, and love is what you are. You are searching for that one moment when you can be fully drunk, intoxicated, in the experience of your own love, the immensity of your own love, with no bondage, with no dependency on anything external - your body, your mind, and the whole world they have created for themselves. True love is the one that can nourish you so completely that you don't have to search for anything else. When you touch that realm of love, when you become love, your life is no longer a searching. It is no longer a chasing. It is no longer trying to turn that image into a reality. It acquires a totally different rhythm. It moves so differently that you might as well be living in a totally different world. That is why the one who is drunk in love and the one who is intellectually chasing after images live in two different worlds. One cannot understand the other.

If you were to tell an intellectual, if you were to explain to him what feeling drunk is, how can you explain it? Imagine if a person has no conception of intoxication, for whatever reason. He has not had anything that has given him that sense of intoxication. He has not drunk alcohol. He has not had sex. He has not experienced a moment of being thrown out of the body accidentally, where he has no conception of his mind and body - where he is reeling in a certain realm. Imagine if such a thing has never happened. If you don't know what being drunk is, how is it possible to explain what being drunk is?

At the most, you can show him someone who's drunk and tell him that he's drunk. He will look at that person from the outside and say, "I don't want to be like that. He's unable to walk. He's talking gibberish. I cannot even understand what he is trying to say. He's a fool. I don't want to be that." The reason why he's unable to understand is because he is only seeing what he is used to seeing. He cannot see anything more than what he is capable of seeing. Unless he knows how to get intoxicated, the one who's intoxicated will look like a fool to him.

That is why, for a worldly man chasing worldly dreams and desires, a mystic, a meditator, someone who's spending his time in silence, in stillness, doing nothing will look like a lunatic - will appear to be a madman. "Look at him. He doesn't look like me. He doesn't move like me. He doesn't talk like me. He doesn't think like me. So he has to be mad because I know I am not mad. If I'm not mad, he has to be mad." The only problem is that the intellectual has not tasted the deeper realms of himself. He's just stuck on the surface, and for him, he cannot imagine anything other than what he's experiencing.

Advice doesn't help lovers!
They're not the kind of mountain stream
you can build a dam across.

An intellectual doesn't know
what the drunk is feeling!

Don't try to figure
what those lost inside love
will do next!

Someone in charge would give up all his power,
if he caught one whiff of the wine musk.
from the room where the lovers
are doing who-knows-what!

You cannot understand. If you were to be given a taste, if you were to be accidentally given a glimpse of that intoxication, you would drop everything you are doing and you would start chasing it. Immediately, you would know that that's the purpose of your life. Your purpose is not to become rich. Your purpose is not to become famous. Your purpose is not safety, security, and all that Man is chasing. You are searching for the purest wine, you are searching for the oldest wine that knows intoxication in ways you cannot even imagine. It has been sitting and fermenting since the beginning of time - it is there in the wine cellar, which is your own body. It is sitting there. You know it. You get a sense of it. You walk around it. Something tells you it is there, but you don't know how to look for it. You don't know how to recognize it. But it is there.

If accidentally, while you are fumbling through all the other bottles - the imaginary bottles with imaginary wine - you happen to find this bottle and if you were to taste it, you would throw away all the other bottles. You would throw away all your other dreams. You would throw away all your other desires because immediately you would know the difference between real and imaginary. You would know this is the real wine. It tastes nothing like all the other drinks you have been having. This is totally different. The intoxication is deep. The bliss is deep. And it feels familiar. It feels very close to yourself.

That is what the worldly man is missing. Once in a while, he hears the words that meditation is the path that leads to that wine cellar, which leads to that ultimate intoxication, his own true being, his own true nature. Intellectually, he can at the most acknowledge it. If he is intelligent enough to realize the futility of his searching on the outside, he will start searching on the inside. If not, he will hear the words but not act on it. He lives in a world of his own.

If only you can be given a glimpse, you will be given access to that sacred temple where there are only lovers. Their ways are different. Who knows what they are doing there? The realm is different. That is why a caterpillar can only dream about what it feels like to be a butterfly. As long as it is a caterpillar, it is crawling on the floor. It does not even know.

THE INTOXICATION OF SLEEP

Life freezes if it doesn't get a taste
of this almond cake.

The stars come up spinning
every night, bewildered in love.
They'd grow tired with that revolving if they weren't.

They'd say,
"How long do we have to do this?

Rumi says that existence is not tired of doing the
same thing again and again, day in and day out,
because it is drunk in love. The stars come to reveal
their drunkenness. Existence is intoxicated. Existence
is filled with that wine of love. That is why it knows
no effort. That is why it knows no boredom, no
worry, no fear. It is living in the world of the drunk.

Existence creates. Purely intellectually, if you look at
it, it is doing a lot of work. But because it is drunk, it
is not work for it. It is just joy. That is what is missing
in man. When he was born, he was very close to the
source. He was reluctantly pulled away from the
source. When he was a baby, he wanted just to sleep

so that he could be as close as possible to the true nature of his being. Sleep was his intoxication.

But eventually, he had to be dragged out. He had to be introduced to the chaos of the world because he had to be made useful. He had to learn many things. He had to become a man of the world. In that process, he forgot what it is to be close to the source. Every day he accidentally falls into that zone, which is what he calls his sleep. If not for sleep, Man would have gone completely mad. That disconnection, that separation from his true nature, would have been so painful. The noise in his head would have been so deafening that he could not have handled it. He would have absolutely gone insane.

The only thing that is keeping human society sane is sleep. No matter what you do, at the end of the day, you have to go to sleep. This is an inbuilt mechanism that is keeping you sane. It reminds you, even without your permission, that it is time to sleep - you have played enough games for the day. It is just a game, but you have taken it too seriously. Existence knows that this creature is only supposed to play for a while and then go back to sleep, back to the source. And no matter who you are, no matter how important your task is, existence will pull you back and say, "go to sleep." That is what is keeping you sane. That is your intoxication.

And what is intoxication at the end of the day? It is to not have to experience the pain of the body and the mind. If something can numb your pain, if something can numb your senses, if your senses can be dulled to a point where they are no longer stinging you, that is intoxication. And when you are asleep, your body is not disturbing you. Your mind is not disturbing you. You are not worried about all the things that you worry about during the day. And that is why you enjoy sleep so much.

There is another kind of sleep - wakeful sleep, known only to a mystic, known only to the one who is drunk in love. He doesn't have to go to sleep to be close to the source. He doesn't have to jump out of his body to experience bliss. He has found the source. He has become the source. For him, he's asleep even while fully awake. A part of him is awake, a part of him is moving, desiring. But another part of him is blissfully asleep. That's why there is no chaos, no confusion, no longing, no searching. He's just there.

Those who pay attention to ways of behaving
and speaking are one sort,
While lovers who burn are another.

When light returns to its source,
it takes nothing
of what it has illuminated.

There are different paths one can take to get to the truth. Many choose the intellectual path because that is where they are at. They want to first understand what a spiritual journey is through their mind. They want explanations. They want to know what it is that they are getting. They want to know what it takes to practice. They want to know the method and the technique. They want to know if the information is coming from a trusted source. They are looking for a perfect explanation that can convince them why they should start searching. They are looking for a flawless explanation. They miss out, because even when they are introduced to that information, the flaws in their own mind somehow make even that flawless information filled with flaws. They see the flaw either in the technique, in the teacher, how long it takes to get there, or what it is that they are going to experience at the end. Somewhere they will find a flaw and use that as a reason not to pursue.

That is why the intellectual path can easily be missed. You can be introduced to it. You can even be dragged along the path a little bit. But eventually, it all depends on you, whether you want to continue walking that path or not. Because it's an intellectual path, you have not allowed anybody to influence you or your decisions - you have taken control. You have taken the responsibility for your realization yourself. So the challenge is how do you hold on to it? How do you not let your flimsy mind interfere with the process and take you away from the path?

THE PATH OF LOVE

The only other way to bypass the mind and not intellectually inquire and still find the truth is to take the path of love. But you cannot think about it. You cannot ask questions. And you cannot make it happen. It has to happen to you.

The path of love is an elevated path. If the path of the mind is taking steps to enlightenment, the path of love is getting on the escalator straight. You just have to get there. You just have to throw yourself on that escalator. You just have to surrender to it, and it will take you there. But that's the hardest part. How do I trust? You cannot ask questions. Either trust has happened or it hasn't. Either love has happened or it hasn't.

The ones who have been touched by love and who pursue the path of love have always reached. There is not a single exception where someone began walking the path of love and gave up in the middle. If they gave up in the middle, then it was never the path of love, because how can you give up when you are not there?

The path of love means that something has become more important than you. That something is drawing you toward it. You can call it by any name: God, divine, eternity, Shiva, Jesus, Buddha. When the connection is direct, when you have no doubt whatsoever in the words they have spoken, when you one hundred percent trust and accept their words as true, you stop searching on your own. You just want to be in the presence of their words, their actions, and their being. Slowly, your thoughts, your dreams, your desires are being replaced by theirs.

It almost seems like madness. "How can I trust someone I don't know? How can I trust something that I have not seen or experienced?" The moment you inquire even this much, you are on the intellectual path. You are no longer on the path of love. Love, when it happens, happens as a force. It happens to the one who is very innocent, who knows nothing about the ways of the world, or to someone who has grown fully tired of the ways of the world. He is looking for something to come and sweep him away.

There are beautiful examples of individuals who have walked the path of love all the way to awakening. In fact, you cannot even say "walk." They have danced their way to enlightenment. A lover does not walk. She dances.

There is a beautiful way of understanding the difference between walking and dancing. What is the difference? What is the fundamental difference between walking and dancing? In walking, you are always going somewhere. You walk to go from one place to another. But in dancing, you have no desire to go anywhere. That is why the path of the lover is a dance, and it is a pathless path. Because your destination is not somewhere else - your destination is the present moment itself.

If you can simply dance and reach such depths of connectedness with your being, when you dance with absolute abandon, without any care in the world, there will come a moment when you will lose body consciousness completely. The ecstasy of dance can take you to such heights that you will drop the last limitation that is holding you back from dancing with no limitation. That is your own body. You can dance with great grace, great intensity with your body, but there will always be a limitation. But when the body is dropped, the dance is universal.

And what is dance? It is to experience a sense of freedom. When you are walking, it is a set pattern. When you are dancing, you are doing something unique. You are moving differently. You are experiencing more freedom when compared to walking. That is what dancing is. When dancing reaches its absolute peak, you will drop all limitations and you will see that even the body is a limitation. You will say, "I want to dance without this limitation," and when that happens, that is when enlightenment happens. That is when awakening happens.

Mirabai danced her way to enlightenment. She had no method, no path, no teacher, no guidance, nothing. Every night, she would go to the temple and dance in front of the statue of Krishna. People thought she was mad. "What is she doing?" they would say. "Every night she goes to the temple and dances in front of a statue." Yes, there was an understanding that it was the statue of Lord Krishna, that he was divine. People understood devotion and worship, but they did not understand love.

For Mira, Krishna was not a person. For her, he was not God. For her, he was her destination. She was so fully in love with him that she did not see anything else other than him. Her thoughts were his thoughts. Her body was his body. She had given herself. She had surrendered herself completely to Krishna. And that surrender did not happen at the end of her journey - it did not happen just before becoming enlightened. That was the starting point of her journey. What an intellectual sees as the beginning of the journey, for her, was the end of the journey.

When she abandoned herself, when she let go of her mind, when she let go of her body, she became enlightened right there. It only took her a little more time for her body to know, for her being to know. She was not even trying to do anything. She had already become a part of Krishna. That is why she was dancing in front of him. She was offering herself to him.

This is hard to understand. For the modern man, it is impossible to understand. For Mira, that is the only life she knows. You only have to get a sense of the innocence, the level of innocence that is required to love with such abandon. There cannot be a single doubtful thought. There cannot be a single question - "What if he's not real?" One doubt, one question - "What if he's not my destination?" - you cannot dance, because doubt has come into your mind.

There are other examples, such as Akka Mahadevi from the South. She was a queen, but when she was touched by love, she devoted herself to Shiva. She left her kingdom and became a wandering mystic. Akka Mahadevi is always depicted in images as a woman who is clothed in her own hair. This might be an exaggeration, but it is a symbolic way of saying that she did not need anything. She did not need any manmade safety or protection. She was complete.

She attained realization not through any method or technique, but because she saw her life ending in Shiva. Shiva was the end of her life. That love, that devotion, which has no room for doubt - the one who walks such a path has always gone all the way. In fact, it is only the intellectual that uses words. She walked the path. She became enlightened. For her, she had already reached.

Love is your destination. If it has happened to you, if you have fallen in love with something, and if you are willing to lose yourself in that love, there is nothing higher than that. If not, search for it. Look for it. Don't let your mind intellectually argue for or against your searching, because your mind is blind. It cannot sense what you are searching for. It is not drunk. It is too logical. It is too structured. It is only chasing after one image after another. It has to be a leap of faith. It is only a matter of time.

THE MIRROR OF CONSCIOUSNESS

You may have heard, it's the custom for kings
to let warriors stand on the left, the side of the heart,
and courage.

On the right, they put the chancellor,
and various secretaries, because the practice
of bookkeeping and writing usually belongs
to the right hand.

In the center, the Sufis,
because in meditation they become mirrors.
The King can look at their faces
and see his original state.

Give the beautiful ones mirrors,
and let them fall in love with themselves.

That way they polish their souls
and kindle remembering in others.

There is this whole idea of left brain and right brain. Scientists say that the left brain is analytical, logical, and deals with language, while the right brain is concerned with intuition and creativity, artistic and musical abilities, and processing of emotions. In a way, the right brain is concerned with creativity, while the left brain is concerned with logic and more structured thinking.

You can look at it as the energies are different. On the left side, the energy moves in steps, looking for validation, just like a computer program. It processes something and checks for validation. Depending on the validation, it moves to the next step. This is what analytical reasoning is. You don't just jump into doing many things. You don't jump in blindly. You watch your step and go slowly. On the other hand, creativity is a direct leap. You're not looking for any validation. You're not comparing your progress. You are looking for something new. You're trying to venture into unknown territory.

While the separation between left and right brain appeals to our desire to understand the inner world, it is a totally arbitrary, flimsy, and silly categorization. There may be some truth to it, but it has been taken too literally.

First, the brain is an extraordinarily complex organ. The left and right hemispheres can only be seen when the head is cut open. In our everyday experience, when we try to be creative, we do not consciously try to stimulate the right side of our brain, or tilt our heads to the right. If creativity were located in the right brain, why would we not do something to stimulate it?

Scientists also say that the right hemisphere of the brain is connected to the left side of the body, and vice versa. Therefore, if we use our right side of the body more, we are stimulating the left side of the brain. This means that if you are right-handed, every time you write with your right hand, you are stimulating your analytical, logical, and reasoning mind. And if you are left-handed, you are stimulating your creative side.

We have had all kinds of examples. We have had examples of individuals who are extraordinarily creative, both left-handed and right-handed. There is no direct correlation between being left-handed and being creative - although it is nice to think in those terms, because most people are right-handed. If you are left-handed, and if somewhere, you have been told that being left-handed makes you more creative because you are stimulating the right side of your brain, you can feel good for a moment, but it is nothing to boast about.

Whether you are using your right hand or left hand is completely arbitrary. The brain is a lot more complex than that. And more importantly, the realm of thoughts is even more complex. If you think the brain is hard to understand, venture into the world of thoughts. Venture into the world of dreams and imagination, and you will see that everything merges - left, right, top, down, center. Sometimes your insides are turned inside out. Outside is turned inside in. Left is becoming right. Right is becoming left. There is nothing sequential there. One object morphs into something else. Your body changes. Suddenly, day changes into night, and night changes into day. In the dream realm, nothing is fixed. In fact, the whole idea of left and right keeps interchanging. Because what is left if not for the other side of right, and what is right if not for the other side of left? When you enter a dream space, left and right can interchange just as easily. It is just our arbitrary way of identifying something.

In reality, these designations do not exist. That is why existence does not know the difference between up and down, left and right. Only in human experience do these differences exist, and we give them importance. However, the further you go away from human experiences and look at existence just the way it is, you will see that all of these concepts fall away.

Apart from left and right, there is a center to our being. A center that has nothing to do with the brain. There are different centers within us, and we can operate from those different centers. We have the mind center, the heart center, the center of silence, the center of stillness, a bliss center, and an awakened center. These centers are in fact everywhere, but they are at a certain depth.

When you are able to access a certain center, when you can find your way to a particular center that is at a deeper level, in a way, all of these centers are arranged in a sequential order. For example, your mind center is on the outside. Your heart center is closer to you than your mind center. The direction is inward. The mind center is the outermost, and then there is the heart center. Then there is the center of silence. Then there is the center of stillness, then a center of relaxation. Then a center of bliss, then a center of absolutely no feeling, no sensation - the sensation of being stoned. And then there is the center of absolute awakening where you are not experiencing anything except for your own pure being. So, if you look at it from the innermost layer to the outermost layer, the disturbance keeps increasing. The agitation keeps increasing. More things are added, more chaos, more confusion.

That is why if you are stuck in the mind center, life appears to be very chaotic, hard to understand, and difficult to deal with. This is the center where most of humanity lives. This is why there is a quest for relaxation, a quest for deeper meaning, a quest for bliss, a quest for happiness, a quest for enlightenment, and a quest for awakening. They are all somewhere inside you, but you are stuck at the outermost layer.

The deeper you go in, the less desire you have to search, because each deeper layer is more satisfying. It is more relaxing because you are getting closer and closer to your true self. It is not hard to understand. The closer you are to home, the more comfortable you feel. And finally, when you are at home, you feel the most comfortable. When you move away from home, the farther you go, the more anxious and disturbed you become because you are in unfamiliar territory. You need concepts and ideas to navigate, and you cannot rely on your intuition.

Let's say you go to a strange place. How do you navigate that strange place without a map? You need maps. Now, when you are using maps written by someone else, there is always the possibility of getting it wrong or misreading the map. That is the whole confusion in life. We are trying to navigate the maze of life using maps drawn by someone else. Sometimes we get it wrong. We take the wrong road that leads to places we don't like. And then we have to retrace our steps. We are unable to use our intuition because we are in unfamiliar territory.

But when you are closest to your being, when you are at home, you don't use maps to navigate from your living room to your kitchen to your bathroom. You don't rely on someone else's opinions and judgments about how to be. At home, you are just yourself. You don't care about the way you dress, the way you walk, the way you think and move - you are totally free to be yourself. And you have navigated that space so much that you don't need maps. You know where things are intuitively. That keeps you grounded, rooted, and relaxed.

Why is Man so disturbed? Why is he searching for meaning? Why is he searching for relaxation? He is in a strange land, and he is trying to navigate that land using maps drawn by someone else. Sometimes he is using a map that was created thousands of years ago, when the landscape was totally different. What the map is showing and the reality that he is living in are two completely different things, but somewhere he has been told that this is the ultimate map. This is the best map. It came from God himself - and he is trying to compare it to his real life. It doesn't make any sense, but he is trying to cram his real experiences into that artificial map.

That is where the conflict arises. There is a religious map, a philosophical map, a scientific map, and a map of your own understanding of what life is - a map of judgments. In all this chaos, your journey is not joyful. It has become chaotic. With every step you take, you are in doubt: Is this the right thing to do? Am I following the right map? What if I'm wrong?

Think about it. Isn't that what the chaos in life is all about? What is the difference between that state and a deep meditative state? In a deep meditative state, you are closer to your being. You have thrown away all the maps. You have stopped listening to people. You have stopped caring for your religious scriptures. You have stopped caring for blind dogmatic beliefs. Now, you have something of your own - your own experience. You have tasted something. You have touched something.

Now, when you are introduced to an idea, you immediately compare it to your internal realm. How does this apply to me? How does this apply to my deepening of the experience of life? Does it help or hurt? Immediately, you will know how to distinguish between knowledge that takes you deeper and information that takes you outside. And if you are able to distinguish that, then all your troubles are gone. You don't have to deal with the chaos of the world anymore. You don't have to deal with the world trying to get your attention constantly, because you have seen and experienced enough to know that they are all living in a state of not knowing.

These maps are written by blind people. They haven't navigated the landscape of life themselves. They have been referring to other maps. So, basically, the map that is given to you is a map of a map of a map. It is not pointing to any real territory.

Now, what happens when one map starts referring to another map? It gets doubly complex. Now you need to understand what this map is trying to say about that map and where that map is pointing to. That's where life gets more and more complicated because instead of experiencing something real, you are only experiencing ideas of ideas. The way out of this chaos is to throw away all the maps and to trust your own experience. That is the only way to find true peace and joy.

You are stuck in a realm of imagination, concepts, and theories. It's natural. You are unable to enjoy the reality of life. You're unable to move intuitively, and most of the time, you're sitting in your room or in the hotel lobby of this strange, beautiful place. You spend the entire day reading the maps and are afraid to go out because unless you figure out the map, you will not have the confidence to do so. The maps are so confusing. You're so tired by the end of the day that you go to sleep. And when you wake up the next day, you pick up the maps again. You spend the whole day in that room and then go to sleep.

By the time you realize, by the time the light starts shining through the window, you're too old. You've lost all your energy, and you're no longer interested in going out. The outside has become too strange a phenomenon. "Meditation, mindfulness, going inward, awakening - it's not for me. I'm happy in this hotel room. At least I know how to move here. At least this much familiarity is there. I know my job, my salary, my friends, and my family members. I know where a restaurant is and where an ATM machine is. That's more than enough."

But what is it that you're missing in this experience? Everything. You're missing life itself. You're missing a deep communion with yourself. You're missing a spectacular experience that has just been waiting there for you. You've been missing bliss. You've been missing joy. You've been missing life itself.

FOCUS ON THE CENTER

In the center, the sufis,
Because in meditation, they become mirrors.

The king can look at their faces
and see his original state.

Give the beautiful ones mirrors,
and let them fall in love with themselves.

That way they polish their souls
and kindle remembering in others.

Rumi says to let those who want to be concerned with
the left, be concerned with the left. Let those who
want to be obsessed with the right, stay with the right.
Routine activities, mental activities that don't really
mean much, simple arrangements. You focus on the
center. The center is where the Sufi is. The center is
where the mystic is. The center is where the seeker is.
He does not care about the left and the right. He
wants to go straight to the heart of understanding.

Now, what is at the center? A mirror. Look at the
beauty, the depth, the level of Rumi's understanding
of the inner dimension of life. Once you start your

journey inward, you will see that you are actually moving closer and closer towards an infinitely pure mirror. A mirror that can reflect everything perfectly. In fact, your consciousness is the most perfect mirror that can ever be created. It is a mirror in every dimension. It is a mirror in every angle. It is a mirror without any edges. It is a mirror not created using materials, but something that has always been there.

Now, what is stopping you? What is blocking your perception of this pure mirror? You are this pure mirror. In fact, without this mirror, there is no way to even know that you exist. When you stand in front of the mirror and look at that image and you tell yourself "that is me," what is happening there? Two levels of reflections are happening right there. One is just the reflection of the physical mirror. Your body, the form is being reflected, and the image is being recorded by you, and that is how you can see the body.

But there is another reflection that is happening there that you are not aware of, but you can become aware of. It is something that is bouncing back and forth between your innermost layer and your outermost layer, reminding you of who you are. In that very moment, when you are looking into the mirror, you are not just looking at your body. You are also telling yourself, "I am that body."

Where does this come from? It comes from the pure nature of consciousness. That is why, wherever you go, apart from reflecting the experiences of the outside world, you are also constantly reflecting on the inside. This is what we call an emotion, a feeling, or a connection. These are all different words we use for a simple, existential phenomenon called reflection.

You are seeing yourself in others. You are seeing yourself in things. When you look at a bird flying in the sky, you are not just looking at an image. You are not just looking at an animated image. You are also seeing yourself in that bird. This is what brings an emotion out of you. How can this happen if you are not a mirror, and that mirror extends all the way from where you are to that bird? Existence itself is a mirror. That is why, wherever you go, the ripples of your being, the ripples of your emotions, and the ripples of your thoughts are being reflected in everything.

That is why, when you see someone suffering, you suffer inside. When you see someone laughing, whether you want to laugh or not, you will laugh. Because there is a mirror inside that reflects everything purely. This mirror can be covered up. It can be burdened with layers and layers of dust to the point where the reflection is no longer pure. The reflection is being filtered through a routine, mechanical, fearful, and structured mind.

That is why Rumi says,

Give the beautiful ones mirrors,
and let them fall in love with themselves.

That way they polish their souls
and kindle remembering in others.

Give them mirrors. Introduce them to their own purity. Introduce them to the pure reflective nature of their being. Let them fall in love with themselves. That is the whole essence of spirituality. It is to fall in love with yourself so completely, so fully, so utterly that you don't need anything else. You become the object of your love.

Whatever is happening on the inside - good, bad, right, wrong - it doesn't matter. Once you unconditionally accept yourself and unconditionally love yourself, your polishing has begun. Only when you don't like yourself or when you hate yourself do you start looking for answers on the outside. Instead of polishing the mirror, you try to find ready-made solutions and ready-made ideas to add to it. Without realizing that it is only when you are able to get rid of the dust that has settled, the dust of ideas, the dust of false maps, and the dust of false instructions, that you can truly fall in love with yourself. You can fall in love with the pure nature of your being.

When you are not introduced to this, you are always on the outside. As a result, when you witness someone suffering, you too, experience an internal sense of suffering. Similarly, when you see someone laughing, even if you resist, the mirror within compels you to laugh as well. This internal mirror reflects everything purely, creating a profound inter-connectedness between you and the world.

The mirror of our being can be obscured and burdened by layers of dust, reaching a point where the reflection is no longer pure. Introducing individuals to their own purity and the reflective nature of their being is essential in spiritual growth. Falling in love with oneself utterly and completely becomes the essence of spirituality - a love so profound that external desires fade away.

By unconditionally accepting and loving oneself, the process of polishing begins. The inner turmoil of good, bad, right, and wrong no longer holds power over the journey of self-discovery. However, if self-doubt or self-hatred exists, individuals tend to seek external solutions, ready-made ideas, or quick fixes to cover up the dust on their mirrors. This approach prevents them from truly falling in love with themselves and embracing the pure essence of their being.

Only by clearing away the settled dust - the dust of false ideas and instructions - can one genuinely fall in love with themselves and their true nature. Without this introduction to inner purity, individuals remain on the periphery, disconnected from their authentic selves, constantly seeking answers outside of themselves. "That way, they polish their souls and kindle remembering in others."

Sufis use a beautiful word for remembering - zikr. Zikr means the remembrance of God, the remembrance of the divine. For Sufis, God is not an anthropomorphic God, a religious God, or a biblical God. God is equality, purity, and consciousness itself. Zikr is a method they use to come back to the true self. It is one of the core teachings of Sufis. In their poetry, in their reflections on life, and in their exploration of love, one constant theme is zikr, or remembering.

Rumi also says something beautiful: "Let them stay at the center. Let them purify that mirror, let them become pure reflections so that the king can see his true face in the mirror." What he is saying is that when you stare into a pure mirror, its purity does not reveal its own nature, but rather reveals who you are.

When you stare into the mirror, you are actually not looking at the mirror. You don't care about the mirror. In fact, you only look at the mirror when there is something wrong with the mirror. If the mirror is broken, dusty, or if you are not able to see the reflection clearly, that is when your attention goes to the mirror. The purer the mirror, the harder it is to see it.

Why is it hard to see consciousness? It is because consciousness is a mirror with no edges. Imagine if you were standing in front of a mirror that extends to infinity in all directions. Wherever you turn, you have that mirror. How would you know you were actually standing in front of a mirror? It is impossible. It is only the imperfections of the mirrors that we stare into in the physical world that make us aware of them. We can see the dust on them, the edges, and we know where the mirror ends. We also know what is not reflecting.

The goal of zikr is to polish the mirror of consciousness until it is so pure that we can see our true selves reflected in it. When we do this, we realize that we are not separate from God or the divine. We are all one, connected in consciousness.

If you were to stand in front of a wall, you would know the difference between standing in front of a mirror and standing in front of a wall. The experience is totally different. And that is how you know that a mirror reflects.

The problem with consciousness is that it is so pure, so complete, and not man-made. It has no edges. There is no way for you not to reflect, so you are always reflecting. The reflection is so complete that you are only thinking about yourself. Morning to evening, day in and day out, this mirror is reflecting you: "How do I look? How do I think? How do I behave? How much have I grown?" - all the things that are concerned with your life. But in this entire process, one thing we are forgetting is the mirror itself that is helping us to see ourselves. Without the existence of that mirror, even such a simple thing as "I am here. I am walking. I am thinking" is impossible. The possibility of reflection is what allows for the possibility of life. And when this mirror is pure, it reflects everything exactly the way it is supposed to be.

Imagine a person standing in front of a king. Let us say that he is just another ordinary citizen of the kingdom. The king asks him a few questions, wanting to know more about himself. Imagine if the king is an absolute idiot. He has no sense of what he is doing, and the person knows this. Would the person tell the king that? No. He knows what the king wants to hear, otherwise his head is in danger. He knows that if he speaks the truth, his life is in danger. So he says things that the king wants to hear.

The king is standing in front of an imperfect mirror, a mirror that is lost in fear, prejudice, and judgment. So the reflection is not pure. Imagine if the individual were to be an enlightened person, an awakened being who has come from a totally different kingdom. He does not care about the king, the kingdom, or living or dying. If he happens to come to the king, and gets to know that the king is not very smart, when the king asks him the question, he will tell the truth - because the king is standing in front of a pure mirror.

What is the difference between the enlightened one and the unenlightened one? They were both reflecting through the same mirror, the mirror of consciousness, the mirror of aliveness. But one had purified their mirror through a process of self-transformation. He had fallen in love with himself and navigated the inner landscape of life enough to eventually remove all the dirt and grime sticking on the mirror. And that is how, when you stand in front of them, you see yourself clearly.

On the other hand, the unenlightened one is living in fear. He is living in his own prejudices and judgments.

- trying to safeguard his body and mind - so he cannot be truly honest with himself.

That is the difference between an enlightened one and an unenlightened one. One is free to be himself. The other is bound to the life that he has accepted for himself. He is living in the world of ideas while the enlightened one is living in reality.

FINDING A SURGEON

There is nothing worse
than thinking you are well enough.
More than anything, self complacency
blocks the workmanship.

Put your vileness up to a mirror and weep.
Get that self satisfaction flowing out of you!
Satan thought, "I am better than Adam,"
and that 'better than' is still strongly in us.

Your stream water may look clean,
but there's unstirred matter on the bottom.
Your sheikh can dig a side channel
that will drain that waste off.

Trust your wound to a teacher's surgery.
Flies collect on a wound. They cover it,
Those flies of your self-protecting feelings,
your love for what you think is yours.

Let a teacher wave away the flies
and put a plaster on the wound.
Don't turn your head. Keep looking
at the bandaged place.
That's where the light enters you.

Rumi is saying that a wound is the place where the light enters. He is talking about the human condition, the sickness that humans are unaware of. He says that it is foolish to think that you are not sick when you are sick. You can cover it up or hide it, but sooner or later, you will have to attend to your sickness. Because by the very nature of any sickness, it cannot just be there without worsening, festering, and becoming infectious. You have to eventually tend to it.

It is better to acknowledge that you are sick and give yourself to the wisdom, knowledge, and awareness of a teacher to cure you. The work of a teacher is no different than the work of a surgeon. There is a malignant growth that has to be removed. This growth is called "you."

The malignant growth that is covering the true nature of your being is the very thing that you affectionately call your life - your thoughts, dreams, desires, body, and your mind. While you attach tremendous meaning to all these things, while you hold on to them as if they are your only identity, Rumi is saying that this is just sickness. This is an additional growth that has happened on your true being. This is not who you are.

This additional growth has to be removed. A surgery is required. What kind of surgery? Meditative surgery, mystical surgery, spiritual surgery. And you cannot do it on your own because you are invested in this sickness. You are too attached to it. You need assistance. You need help. The teacher is there to help you remove this malignant growth. He is there to help you see your true nature. He is there to help you become free.

Drop your ego. Become humble enough to accept and understand that you need help. Then, look for a teacher. This is the sad part of modernization: Man has become so self-centered. He has gained enough independence to think on his own, act on his own, and shape his life on his own - to such an extent that he has become arrogant and now refuses to even take the help of a teacher. He sees help coming from outside as a conflict with his own ego.

Someone is willing to help. Someone has navigated the landscape of life. Someone has experienced the deeper truths of life, and they are willing to offer their teachings. If you are willing to humble yourself and accept help, you can find a teacher who can help you on your journey. Throughout human history, there have always been individuals who were willing to pour out their heart and being to help others. The problem has always been with the students. Most of us have not been ready to accept the teacher. We have rejected teachers because we do not want to accept that we are sick.

If you were to approach a believing Christian who has fully accepted that Jesus is his savior and that he has done enough to please him and that he is going to heaven after his death - if he is living in such ideas, and if you were to tell him, "This is sickness. These are not real ideas. You have been tricked into believing this, or you are invested in these ideas. Recognize that you are sick. Listen to Buddha. Listen to Jesus' true words. Listen to an awakened one. Listen to the teachers - not the preachers," Immediately, he would reject that information because it clashes with his ego.

The preachers have satisfied his ego. That was their work. Every time he goes into the church, every time he is introduced to the religious scriptures, his ego is satisfied because he did not have to do anything. He is being told every moment that just by accepting Jesus, just by believing in him, just by coming to the church, just by being a Christian, everything else is taken care of. So, the ego has no necessity to work on itself and transcend it. There is no possibility for him to see his sickness. He will continue to be sick. He will continue to live in that realm of unawareness, unconsciousness, and ignorance, believing all the while that he is healthy.

What is stopping him from turning towards a teacher? It is the ego. It is not that he hasn't heard words of purity. It is not that he has not seen a deeper meaning in the words of Jesus or Buddha. It is not that an awakened man's teachings have not resonated in his being, they have. He has blocked it because he is too self-centered and attached to his pride to accept the fact that he has been sick for such a long time.

The ego is a powerful force. It is the root of all our suffering. It is the thing that keeps us from seeing the truth. It is the thing that keeps us from being free. If we want to be free, we must transcend the ego. We must become humble. We must become open to learning. We must become willing to let go of our attachments. If we do this, we will find the teacher we are looking for. We will find the path to freedom.

Not only has the individual been sick - his community has been sick, his preachers have been sick. The whole religious structure has been nothing but a cancerous growth. It is not healthy. It is filled with blood and pus. The reason he is not able to see it is because the wound is still covered up. He can feel the pain. That is why a religious person, as much as he appears to be safe and secure on the outside - when he is a part of his community and singing religious songs or chanting religious scriptures - when he is alone, he feels lost. He cries in pain. In fact, a religious man suffers more than a non-religious man. Because at least for the one who is not stuck in all those religious ideas, the confusion is real. The chaos of life is real. And he is trying to understand it. But for the one who has believed for such a long time that he does not have to do anything, that he is saved, and yet he is going through all these problems, it is a shock.

Imagine you trust that the God you believe in is taking care of you. You fully trust him. And then you wake up one day and you are told that you have some kind of a terminal disease. Your whole belief is shattered. Now why you? Why not your atheist neighbor? If anybody, he was supposed to get that disease because he did not believe in God, he did not go to church, and he is happy going about his life. Why me?

This is the question that every religious person asks himself at some point in his life, and there is no answer. There is no answer that will satisfy you. The only answer is to let go of your belief in God and to start living your life based on your own experience. The only answer is to become free.

Well, you have been living in a world of ideas. And then, for whatever reason, you lose some of your wealth, or your health, or your loved ones. This confusion, every challenge, every obstacle, which is a natural part of living, hits you, and your faith is questioned. Doubt arises. Naturally, your suffering is more than the suffering of a non-believer.

Why? Because your ego is now intermixed with the ego of your community, of your religion, of a religion that has thousands of years of history. Now, if you have to drop your ego and take the help of a teacher, you have to drop something very heavy. You have to drop so much more than just your own mind and body. You have to drop an artificially inflated ego that is your whole world.

But to the one who can recognize, it doesn't matter. "It doesn't matter if my world is big, complex, enticing, or exciting. The moment I recognize that it is a malignant growth, I should have the intelligence enough to say, 'This is too much for me to deal with. I need the help of someone who has performed the surgery already. Yes, I can do the surgery myself, but it is very painful. And it is easy for me to give up somewhere midway. Initially, yes, I might recognize that this is not me. All these ideas have been added to my being. I want to get rid of this, and I want to meditate. I want to awaken myself.'" But without the help of a teacher, without the help of the scriptures, it is easy to get stuck somewhere in the middle. It is easy to become complacent. It is easy to take wrong paths.

If you are ready to let go of your ego and to seek help from a teacher, then you are on the path to freedom. That is why the simplest way to go beyond sickness is to go to a doctor or a surgeon. That is their job. They have dedicated their lives to learning how to remove this growth. While you were sitting and accumulating this malignant growth, they were figuring out how to remove it. While you were only adding to your problems, they were figuring out how to take it out. That is their work. Why not make use of their work?

Just as it is stupid to say, "When I am sick, when my body is sick, I am going to heal it by myself. I will not go to the doctor. I will not go to an expert." It is the same thing as saying, "I will not go to a teacher. I will not go to an expert. I will not listen to someone else." But that is the sad state of the world. People are filled with their own egos to such a level that even asking for help seems ego-destroying. But that is the way. You have to be willing to put yourself on the surgery table and allow the teacher to operate on you. You have to be willing to surrender to the knowledge, wisdom, and understanding of the teacher.

And again, you do not have to blindly surrender. Unlike religions, here you have your mind. The teacher never takes away your mind. He never takes away your body. He adds to your understanding. He teaches in a way that you can understand and navigate.

How do you know you are in the presence of a teacher who is actually helping you to go beyond sickness? You are able to go beyond sickness yourself. You are able to understand yourself. So you do not need blind faith. You do not need blind trust. But you do need to recognize the sickness. The teacher is there to help you see the truth. He is there to help you remove the malignant growth that is covering your true nature. He is there to help you become free.

The Whirling Dervish

WHAT ARE YOU SEARCHING FOR?

When you are searching for something, you are also limiting yourself by believing that you know what you are searching for. Otherwise, how could you search? In searching, there is an assumption that you have some idea of what you are searching for. But in longing, you have no idea. You are longing for something that you cannot even put into words. That is why you cannot talk about it, you cannot think about it, and you cannot share it. You can only be with it in silence or sing it as an expression of poetry.

Rumi is going to the very heart of the search when he says, "**Why should I seek? I am the same as he.**" He is looking at the one who is searching and saying, "What are you searching for? What is the need to search? You are what you are searching for."

It is only when you stop searching that you can find what you are searching for. It is your search that is creating distance between you and what you are searching for. It is your search that is taking you away from yourself.

All those who have found what they are searching for have found it within themselves. There is not a single awakened being who has spoken about the ultimate as something totally separate from them. They have always referred to it as an extension of their own being.

Even Buddha, when he said "Nirvana, nothingness," was only referring to the nothingness of experiencing. There is nothing to experience there. There is no mind. There is no body. He did not want to give a word to that thing that he had become. But we can understand through his words that he experienced nothingness, and he came back from that realm to talk about nothingness. This means that the only thing that was left there was him.

When Buddha says that Nirvana is nothingness and there is nothing to experience, we can see that the only thing that has remained is your own true self. Even Buddha, who seems to completely contradict the self by saying that there is no such thing as self, has somehow indicated the existence of the self through his words and his use of the word 'Nirvana.'

Hindu mystics have always used the word 'Self,' 'Aham brahmasmi.' Ramana Maharshi called the ultimate as simply the self. So if you were to ask him any question, he would just say, "Who is asking this question?" His entire method, his entire path was self-inquiry. Don't worry about what; worry about who. Who is searching? Who is seeking? Who is the one asking this question? Who is the one who is lost? Who is the one who is looking for answers? Because that is the one you are searching for. That one cannot be far away from you. It has to be you.

This seems very paradoxical. Now, what do I do? If I am what I am searching for, and if search is pointless, if search is futile, then all I have to do is just accept the fact that I am the one I am searching for. Just simply state right there that I am the objective of my search; I am the destination of my search. And what am I? A limitless being? Is that enough? Just claiming that you are the ultimate, that there is nothing more to see, there is nothing more to search - is that enough? No, it isn't.

Because you either are longing or you have to be searching. Rumi is longing. For the one who is longing, there is no search. He can say, "There is no separation between me and him." But if you are on a path of seeking, if you are not drunk in love, if you are still stuck in your mind, if you are still finding a way out of your mind, then you cannot simply assert that you are the self and stop searching.

In fact, a lot of people have made this mistake because such language exists in the spiritual realm. It is easy to conclude that there is nothing to search. Ramana Maharshi says there is nothing to search. Rumi says there is nothing to search. Buddha says the ultimate experience is Nirvana. "Then why am I wasting my time meditating? Why am I wasting my time searching for something that I already have?" This gives the perfect excuse for the mind to say, "You have already arrived. This is the understanding that you were looking for. Not many people understand this, but you understand it. You have become spiritual. You have realized the ultimate because you know that there is nothing more to seek."

However, this is not the case. There is still a path to be walked, a journey to be taken. Even if you know that you are the ultimate, you still have to integrate that knowledge into your life. You still have to let go of your attachments and your ego. You still have to become one with the world around you.

So, if you are on a path of seeking, do not give up. Do not be fooled by the language of the spiritual realm. There is still much to learn and experience.

For example, U.G. Krishnamurti took this negation to such an extreme level that he stopped all kinds of searching, including spiritual searching and searching for your true self. He took the idea quite literally that there is nothing to search. All search has been added to you from the outside. You yourself cannot search.

He looked at the human mechanism as very primal, as something animal. He said that your anger, your fear, and your desires are not yours. Your body is simply trying to throw those things out. You are not angry. You are not frustrated. If you watch during those moments, you will see that your body does not like that experience and is just trying to throw it out. And you are holding on to it.

Krishnamurti said that the only way to free yourself from these negative emotions is to simply stop holding on to them. Do not resist them. Do not try to change them. Just watch them come and go. And eventually, they will lose their power over you.

This is a very radical approach, and it is not for everyone. But it is worth considering if you are struggling with negative emotions that are holding you back. At a certain level, he is right. The body is simple. It is interested in such simple things as food, rest, sex, comfort, living, and dying. It is not interested in philosophy, in searching for the truth, or in searching for the ultimate.

This is because he has taken the idea that there is nothing to search quite literally. Many others have fallen into the same trap. They start meditating and exploring, and when the journey gets difficult, they start finding solace in such words: "There is nothing to search."

Rumi himself says, "Why should I seek? I am the same as he. His essence speaks through me. I have been looking for myself." But observe how he is saying this. He is not saying this from his mind. This is the language of the heart. He does not want to search because he wants to be with the one he is searching for. He knows how to be. He knows love. He knows union. He knows longing.

So for him, search is useless. But for you, search is an absolute necessity because you are in the mind. Rumi has already transcended his mind. That is why his poetry cannot be understood intellectually. If you try to break his poetry down intellectually, it will not make any sense because he is ending your search even before it begins.

And yet, he is an awakened soul. He is a realized being. And in his poetry, he wants you to experience what he has experienced. But he is telling you not to search. This seems like a contradiction, but the contradiction is only because he is speaking the language of the heart. You are listening through your mind. To listen to Rumi, you need to throw away your mind and look at his poetry from a space of emptiness where there are no forms, no images. Where there is nothing moving, no shadows, no reflections. There is just pure experience of the now.

This is not easy to do, but it is possible. And it is the only way to truly understand Rumi's poetry. That is what he is talking about. If you can be in the present moment, there is no need to search. In fact, your search is simply a way of being. It is simply a way of connecting with that being that is here right now, because you and what you are searching for are not two different things. They are one and the same.

There is nothing to seek. You only have to realize. There is a difference between finding something and realizing it. Because spiritual awakening is a realization, there is nothing to seek. If what you are searching for were to be anywhere else, other than where you are. If it were to be separate from you, then seeking and searching would make sense. But if something is simply covering up the truth, if something is just blocking it, then it is just a matter of realizing. So where would you go searching?

Just imagine you are the sky and you have identified fully with the clouds. You have forgotten that you are the sky, but you are the sky. You are sitting on the cloud and you are searching for the sky. Now, wherever the cloud goes, you are moving with it. And you are seeing everything through that cloud. And you have mistaken yourself to be that cloud. you are searching for the sky.

When will you become the sky? It is not when you can travel far enough on that cloud. It is not when you can travel fast enough on that cloud. It is when you can simply realize that it is that cloud, the very cloud that on which you are sitting that is blocking your view of the sky.

Existentially, nothing is separating you from the sky. In fact, even though you are identified with the cloud, even though you are sitting on the cloud, the cloud also belongs to the sky because the sky is not an image. The sky encompasses everything, including the clouds. So you are never out of the sky. But you are trying to realize the sky. In a way, you have identified yourself with something limited, which is your mind and your body. You are trying to experience the limitless.

This limitless does not need to be manifested. You do not have to create it. You are already that. It is only a matter of realizing. Now, here is the tricky part. How do you realize? You might think that all you have to do is simply realize. You might say, "Okay, let me realize it." But what is the difficulty? The problem is with words. We use the word "realize" in a very shallow sense. For example, we might say, "Oh, I just realized where I left my bag." In this context, we are using the word "realize" purely in the intellectual realm.

However, the realization that is needed in the spiritual realm is not intellectual, but existential. There is another part of you, apart from your mind, that has to realize experientially that you are not the body. This is why enlightenment is not as simple as just intellectually realizing that you are enlightened. It is not as simple as intellectually accepting that you are the self, or just intellectually saying, "I am everything. I am Brahman."

Enlightenment has nothing to do with what you are telling yourself. It has something to do with what you are experiencing. Have you experienced a single moment when you were not the body? When you were there, but there was no body? If you have experienced this, then you have had a moment of realization. This is because it is an existential experience. Existentially, you have become something other than the body.

As long as you are stuck in the body, as long as you are sitting in meditation, as long as the explosion has not happened, as long as the mind and body have not fully evaporated, you have not yet realized. You have to search. If you are using your mind, you are searching. If you are using your heart, you are longing.

Try and be a sheet of paper with nothing on it.
Be a spot of ground where nothing is growing,
where something might be planted, a seed,
possibly from the absolute.

He says that all you have to do is be empty, be hollow. Get rid of your thoughts, get rid of your desires. Get rid of searching and seeking. Rumi is offering a path to direct enlightenment. It takes great courage to do this, but if you can do it, the realization is right there. If you can be blank, then the seed will be planted. The seed of the absolute. And what is the absolute? Your own true nature, your own self.

How do you get rid of the writing, how do you get rid of the stories that you've been telling yourself? That is the tricky part. That is the seeker's journey. Your journey is not to go somewhere. Your journey is not to find something. Your journey is how to erase yourself. How to become less and less until you reach a point where you are flipping through the pages of your life and they are only blank pages. There is nothing to read. You have forgotten about your birth. You have forgotten about all your likes and desires. You have forgotten about the source from which you came. You have forgotten about your parents. You have forgotten about their parents. You have forgotten about all the influences that have shaped you. You are not worried about dying. You are not contemplating death.

You can only be blank in the present moment. In all other moments, you are caught up in the story of your life. The whole trick is learning how to move from the story to silence. When you watch your life, you are seeing nothing but your own understanding of what your life was. Not even what it is. You are simply seeing a story that has already been told. You have told yourself the story of your life. You have narrated it to yourself in a certain way, and that is what you keep listening to. And that is what creates images. That is what creates experiences. That is what pushes you into the experience of life.

For a few moments, if you can stop listening, if there is nothing to listen to, if there is only silence and blankness, then the seed of the absolute will be planted. You are clearing the ground. You are making it fertile for the seed to be planted. It is in the very nature of things.

The moment nature sees that there is fertile ground for the seed of truth, for the seed of awakening to be planted, it will not hesitate to sow the seed. That is why it is impossible for you not to become enlightened if you are open and empty enough in a single moment. It is in the very nature of things to fill you with the deepest understanding of life when you have not corrupted the present moment with your own flimsy understanding of life.

So existence waits. As long as you are telling your own story, it will wait. Because two stories cannot accommodate a single moment. It can either be your story or the true story of your life. Just like you sit and wait in meditation, there is someone waiting with you. There is someone watching your meditation. There is someone watching everything you are doing. If you pay close attention, you can sometimes connect with that watcher. He does not want to miss a single moment of what you are doing. And what is he waiting for? He is waiting for that one moment of absolute silence, absolute stillness, absolute emptiness, so that he can jump in and reveal himself. That is what existence is waiting for.

It is waiting and watching every creature grow and go about its life, hoping that somewhere it will stop. And in most creatures, it is only a disappointment because the unconsciousness is too deep. Even in human beings, unconsciousness is deep. For most people, it will keep on waiting and eventually life ends, and it will continue to wait in the next life. But once in a while, one individual becomes empty enough. That was his practice. That was his meditation: to be empty, to be hollow. Then, in that one moment when you are not telling anything to yourself, when there is that gap between two thoughts, if that gap is long enough, in a few moments, your true self reveals itself.

Be a spot of ground where nothing is growing. Where something might be planted,
a seed possibly from the absolute.

That for one breath, or half breath,
I belong to myself?

As much as a pen knows what it's writing
or the ball can guess, where it's going next.

There is a way between voice and presence
where information flows.

In disciplined silence, it opens.
With wandering talk, it closes.

We are born blank, The slate is clean. But very quickly someone starts writing on it. And very quickly, you assume that you are the one who's writing. And very quickly, you forget the slate. You are so occupied with the writing and the meaning of that writing that you totally forget this writing is happening on a blank canvas. You're so busy trying to follow through on the trail of your story that you forget the screen on which the story is projected. Your body, your mind, all your experiences put together are on one side. They are the writing. The blankness of the paper, the emptiness of the moment, the hollowness on which your mind and body are happening is what you're searching for.

"In disciplined silence, it opens. With wandering talk, it closes." The possibility is right there, but you have to be silent to realize it. And not any silence, disciplined silence. He's drunk. He's in love. He's lost. And yet, he's using the word discipline because the searching cannot be haphazard. It cannot be unconscious momentary silence that happened automatically. It has to be a form of cultivated silence. Silence that you were longing for, you were searching for. There has to be a discipline in cultivating that silence. "In wandering talk, it closes." What is the wandering talk? Your mind. It's always wandering. It's always talking. And that is why being so close to the truth, it has no conception of it. It talks about it, thinks about it, dreams about it, It pushes you into all kinds of desires in the hopes of finding it, but it can never realize it. Because that wandering itself is the blocking.

You need to stop moving. You need to stop talking. You need to be in the here and now to realize the truth. There is a space between the noise of the mind and the silence of presence. There is a space between disciplined silence and wandering talk. That is where you belong. You have to cultivate silence, but you are not just silence. You are something more.

You have to move away from the noise because you are not the noise. You are somewhere in the middle. You are in the middle of everything that is happening. You are everything except everything that you are perceiving. You are the totality of this experience minus what you are experiencing.

So, for a single moment, if you can stop experiencing, if you can stop seeing, if you can stop searching, if you can stop being, you will become what you are searching for.

If what you are searching for is abundant, is all around you, is inside you, is outside you, then there is no way to find it by searching for it. The only way to find it is to realize it - and know what the obstacles are for that realization, clearing out those obstacles, keeping your mind empty, keeping your thoughts free of desires, coming back to the now from the past and the future, and stop wondering. And then, when you are ready and waiting, it will happen. The realization will happen.

THE VEIL OF THE MIND

Out beyond ideas of wrongdoing and rightdoing,
there is a field.
I'll meet you there.

When the soul lies down in that grass,
the world is too full to talk about.
Ideas, language, even the phrase 'each other'
doesn't make any sense.

Man has lived in conflict for a very long time. His life is a bundle of contradictions that he is trying to reconcile. The primary contradiction is his self-identity. There is no one coherent, single, identifiable, relatable reality for him. Every day he wakes up to new thoughts and new dreams. There is a sense of connectedness, but many things are simply floating around, disconnected, and disembodied.

Because he is a vast unknown, everything else is a mystery. Because he cannot see the inside clearly, the outside is hidden as well. What he sees on the outside, what he recognizes as his reality, is disconnected, fragmented, and problematic. Man cannot see what is on the outside without bringing the inside because both are connected. Perception is happening on the inside. The stimulus is outside. The triggers are outside, but the experience is all internal.

And yet, he has lived in a world believing that there is no inside. He has no conception of the inside. Hence, his world has been totally chaotic. Whatever he has tried to create with good intentions, with the desire to understand more about himself and the world he is living in, he has done so in darkness. That is why his structures never extend beyond his immediate time frame or his immediate experiences. Every few generations or so, his entire social structure has to be overhauled, replaced, and re-examined.

So by the very nature of how Man lives, he has created a world that supports that internal ignorance. In fact, the world is a cover-up to hide that he does not know. Without that cover-up, he cannot do anything else other than search for his highest self. It is this cover-up that takes him away from the search and keeps him engaged in things that appear to be useful and meaningful. But in reality, he is just circling in darkness. He does not know where he is going.

It's four a.m. Nazruddin leaves the tavern and walks the town aimlessly. A policeman stops him - "Why are you out wandering the streets in the middle of the night?" "Sir," replies Nazruddin, "If I knew the answer to that question, I would have been home hours ago."

Man is on the outside, struggling to find meaning. He struggles to understand the nature of reality, his mind, and his body because he does not know that he is wandering. He does not know that he has stepped away from home, and he does not know the way back. He has gone so deep into covering up his true identity that he has done it by using names, structures, imaginary concepts, and theories. He is so lost in all of them that he does not even know that he is searching for home and for himself. He spends his entire life looking for things on the outside without realizing that he is walking in the wrong direction.

That is why the farther he goes away from home, the faster he goes. The more sophisticated and advanced his ways of going out become, the more lost he becomes, and the world is a perfect reflection of that.

You can tell that Man is going somewhere because he is not content with the now. How do we know that he is not content with the now? Because he does not talk about the now. He does not reflect on the now. If you listen to the mind of Man, it is always somewhere else.

He truly believes that his life will get better with time and that the life he is searching for, that peace, that certainty, is somewhere out there in the future. He truly believes that he has to go there and get to that place. He does not realize that that is the illusion, the Maya, of life. He is living in a world that he has created through the process of self-hypnosis. He has created the world through his ability to give suggestions to himself. He does not know that he has so much power within him to create things on the outside just by believing, just by suggesting to himself that they exist.

There was an interesting study conducted to understand how the mind creates false memories. Things that aren't even there. The study involved individuals who were instructed to listen to things and watch simple experiences. For example, they were sitting and watching a car drive by. Subconsciously, they were also given instructions on what was happening. For example, they heard a sound that said, "Watch out for the traffic signal. Watch out for the light." This suggestion was only auditory, but when the individuals recorded their experiences, they actually saw these lights in their minds. Visually, the lights were not present, but in their minds, they were there.

This was an intriguing experiment because from the outside, everything seemed normal. The individual was just sitting there and looking at a car driving by. But when the researchers studied the individual's mind, they saw that the mind had replaced the simple image with the words. The mind had picked up signals and other things that were purely imaginary and added them to the experience.

This suggests that we do not store our memories exactly the way we receive them. We add to them. We are constantly manipulating our memories in a way that coincides with and supports our internal belief systems.

It is alarming when you think about it. We used to think that the human body and mind are precise mechanisms that can only perceive things in a certain way. For example, if you created a machine that can see, hear, and perceive reality outside, you could be sure that all machines would perceive the same thing if they were given similar experiences. They would see and hear the same thing because they are going through the same experiences and the underlying mechanism of perception is the same.

However, we have come to understand that human beings are much more complex than that. We do not simply perceive things. We always bring things from the depths of our being, such as our past prejudices, unresolved conflicts, and unresolved emotions, to the surface when we perceive and store memories. In a way, when we look at things, we are not even looking at things the way they are. We are looking at things the way we are.

This suggests that Man is mostly inside, but he does not know this. Because he does not know this, he keeps wondering. He is actually chasing his own shadows. He is chasing his own internal conflicts. He is having a conversation with himself. He is simply using the mind and the experiences of the mind. So he is using the images, the sounds, and his worldly experiences, but he is only seeing what he wants to see. In a way, he is deeply lost in a world of his own. But he lives believing that he is stuck in an alien world.

While everything he sees around him is telling him something and pointing him in a certain direction, he does not believe in the inner world. He sees all these things as things that are happening outside, so he tries to change them on the outside. That is why he keeps on altering his environment. That is why he is never satisfied with the outside. He has been doing this for thousands of years in the hope that one day he can achieve that perfect external reality where he can live without any conflict.

If he truly understands the nature of reality, he will stop all that pointless reconstruction of his environment and realize that whatever he is searching for is right here. The outside is just a play.

The Whirling Dervish

THE JOURNEY OF SELF-DISCOVERY

Life is not a problem to be solved. It is just an experience. Your external environment exists for you to play in. It is a playground with a few more toys, a few more opportunities for excitement, and a few more opportunities for engagement. However, that is not the place where you can find meaning for your life. Either you have found the meaning inside yourself, independent of the social structure, or you are living in ignorance. There is no in between.

For the one who has found the meaning inside, the world is a beautiful place. Even conflicts are engaging and entertaining for him. This is because he is not trying to find himself by resolving those conflicts. He is resolving those conflicts for the sheer joy of it. He is solving problems not to find himself, but simply for the sheer excitement of solving something.

He will continue to create. He will continue to move into the future. This is in the very nature of the human mechanism. He will continue to build and to imagine. However, he will do it not from a space of uncertainty, confusion, and chaos, but from a space of awareness and knowing. When a man knows himself, what he creates is more meaningful because there is no search for meaning. There is only sharing and connecting.

We live in a world where it takes a lot of time for two individuals to connect with each other. We start out as absolute strangers, and that strangeness always remains. No matter how much we try to accept the other as part of our lives, accept the people in our communities, accept the people in our countries or the world, and live without any prejudices, without any discrimination, without any hate or anger, no matter how much we try, there is always something separating us from the other.

This is because we lack a fundamental understanding of who we are. Because we don't know who we are, we can never know the other. So we will always be fearful of the other. This is what we see reflected as anger, discrimination, and intolerance. There is no basis for any form of discrimination, but it is ingrained in humans because they are, in a way, discriminatory towards themselves. They have not fully reconciled with themselves. There are parts of themselves that they like, and there are parts of themselves that they don't like. And that is what they see in the world.

When they reject something, when they show their anger towards something, a group of people, their way of thinking, or their way of living, it has nothing to do with them. They are fighting with their own fears. They are fighting with those parts of themselves that they have not reconciled.

So how can we live in harmony? How can the world become peaceful when there is so much conflict within humans? Unfortunately, we are not addressing this problem. We think the problem is between us, not within us. If there is a conflict between whites and blacks, we look for the conflict between them. We don't go inside and see that the rejection is happening within, not outside. The social structure is only being used to express the rejection. It is only helping to give voice to what you are feeling inside. It is providing you a platform to share your dislike. But the dislike is inside. Racism is totally an internal phenomenon. That is why it is very individualistic.

We can see this in children. Children are not racist. They do not hate each other based on their beliefs, their likes and dislikes, their religious affiliation, which country they are from, or whether their parents are rich or poor. They do not care about all that. They only look at how they treat each other. If another child treats them well, shows them love, and shows them affection, there is no hate. The response is automatically one of love. There is no additional layering that adds to the prejudice.

However, as the child grows up, they are exposed to an environment of conflict. They may also be internally conflicted themselves. Over time, all of these ideas stack up. Eventually, even without their awareness, they have become a bundle of contradictions that they see in the world. They give these contradictions a name, even though they have nothing to do with their inner selves. They make it into an idea: "Oh, the world is filled with all kinds of discrimination. Something has gone wrong." Yes, something has gone wrong. But it has not gone wrong on the outside. It has gone wrong on the inside. They have moved away from themselves.

That is why Rumi says that you have to get to the place where even the word, even the phrase "each other" does not make any sense. You are experiencing the oneness of life so fully, so completely, that there is no necessity to even think of the other as other. What happens when you are operating from that place of oneness? The other is simply an engagement, an entertainment, a conversation, and excitement. It is not a place where you search for meaning.

The starting point of all conflicts is an individual searching for the meaning of their life in the lives of others. And that is where discrimination comes from. That is where anger comes from, because they have attached so much meaning to a certain way of life. They have attached so much meaning to the forms of life.

When there is contradiction in the forms, when they see someone behaving differently, when they see someone with different belief systems, when they see someone who looks differently, who walks differently, who talks differently, because they are searching for meaning on the outside, they see a big conflict and they want to dismiss it. They want to condemn it. They want to push it away. And that is where hatred comes from.

There is no possibility of hatred when you are not searching for meaning on the outside. But as long as you are searching for yourself on the outside, firstly, you will not find it. Secondly, because you are not finding it, you will be frustrated, and you will take that frustration out on all that does not conform to your fixed, rigid, one-pointed understanding of life.

That is why there is no rest for humans. There is no rest for humanity until it turns inside out and becomes spiritual. As of now, everything is flowing from the outside. All the discussions are about the outside. And by the very nature of things, it is the law of nature that things don't flow outside in. They flow inside out.

If you don't have something inside you, you cannot give it. The world is a place to give, not to take. If you walk into the world with any intention of taking, you are inevitably on the path of destruction. Your own destruction, as well as the destruction of the fragility of life. Every step you take, you will be trampling on the delicate balance of life. Because all creatures of existence are created as an expression to give, not to take.

Observe nature. Nature takes so little compared to how much it is willing to give. Every creature of existence takes only as much as is necessary for it to survive. Once that basic survival need is taken care of, it is in the mode of giving. A few hours every day, it is trying to take and the rest of its entire energies are in giving. Look at the tree. Yes, it needs nourishment. It takes something from the earth, but it also gives back in return: fruits, flowers, shade, and oxygen. This is the nature of things, and this is what humans are meant to be like. We are meant to take what we need to survive, but we should also be in a mode of giving.

However, humans have walked into the world with the intention of taking. They do not interact with the world in a way that gives back. They do not even

know what to give because they think they are
beggars. They think they have nothing. They have not
seen the treasures hidden within themselves. They
have not seen the fountain of love that is within
them. They have not seen the seamless realm of
oneness that is within them. They have not seen that
they are complete inside.

Because they have not seen this, they walk into the
world trying to grasp things, trying to grab things,
trying to possess things. This is where all conflict lies.
Life is not designed for possession or grabbing. When
you start doing these things, you invariably hurt
others. You create a lot of pain for other creatures of
existence.

Even theoretically, you can see that you have to take
something from someone in order to get anything. As
long as you are searching for meaning on the outside,
there will be conflict. This conflict is what gets
reflected in everything you do.

The levels of creation are straws in that ocean.
The movement of the straws
comes from an agitation in the water.

When the ocean wants the straws calm,
it sends them close to shore.

When it wants them back in the deep surge,

it does with them as the wind does with the grasses. This never ends.

We know separation so well because we have tasted the union.

The reed flute makes music because it has already experienced changing mud and rain and light into sugarcane.

Longing becomes more poignant if in the distance you can't tell whether your friend is going away or coming back.

The pushing away pulls you in.

Rumi is saying that creation is not a matter of doing, but a matter of happening. There is an underlying ocean of reality that supports everything. What we see on the surface of life are mere reflections, mere ripples, just a few waves here and there. What we are missing is the ocean. What we are missing is the realization that there is something inside us that is complete and all-encompassing. I am simply a reflection in the endless stream of life. There is nothing to hold on to, nothing to grasp. I am a part of a changing phenomenon. And the only way I can find certainty is by accepting that I am change. My body belongs to change, my mind belongs to change. There is no need to cling to experiences.

How can you enjoy a moment when you are trying to cling to it? How can you enjoy an experience when you are afraid of losing it? How can you rejoice in your youth when you are worried about old age? How can you rejoice in your wealth when you are afraid of losing it? You are in a constant state of agitation because the fear of losing is always there. And what is the fear of losing? All that you think you are, but you are not. That is why there is fear.

You have accumulated a lot of ideas about yourself, but no real experience. You have not been shown the way to experience life in totality. You have only been given instructions to look for the signposts of light. There is a signpost that says 'peace.' There is a signpost that says 'happiness.' There is a signpost that says 'success and accomplishment.' And you have been given instructions on how to find that signpost. But inside, you have moved towards the signpost believing that that is your destination. You put in all the effort, you rearrange your life, you work hard, and you get to that signpost. And it says peace and there is an arrow mark. You are like, "Where is peace? I thought if I can just accomplish this, I would find peace." But only when you accomplish it, do you realize that there is no peace to be found there.

The direction is in the opposite. It says, "Go back to where you came from. You have wasted so much of your time going away from the very thing you were searching for." It is a simple realization that we are living in a world of change and that change is not in our control. We are a part of a very deep and vast tapestry of life. Our minds and bodies are infinitesimally small, so small that they are almost irrelevant compared to the aliveness, the consciousness, the light that is holding everything together. That is what moves everything. It moves without wanting to move.

In a way, we are all the changing moods of existence. It is how she wants to experience this moment. She just uses the mind and the body. There are moments when she is happy, and there are moments when she is agitated. And we are all vibrations helping her to experience the wide range of emotions. That is why we experience all that. That is why we experience the entire range of emotions. There is nothing lacking there. But because we are clinging to the experiences, we are unable to let them go.

THE ULTIMATE UNION

A naked man jumps in the river,
hornets swarming above him.
The water is the zikr,
remembering. There is no reality but God.
There is only God.

The hornets are his sexual rememberings.
This woman, that woman.
Or if a woman, this man, that man.
The head comes up, they sting.

Breathe water, become a river head to foot.
Hornets leave you alone then.
Even if you are far from the river,
they pay no attention.

Rumi is talking about the single biggest obsession of humankind: sex. How do you understand it? How do you deal with the desire for sex? What do you do with it? Is there a way to go beyond it? He compares the pangs of sexual desire to the stings of hornets. In a way, this is an apt comparison. Every time you fall into the grip of a sexual desire, two things happen. First, there is a brief period of elation and excitement. There is a lot of activity, along with deep unconsciousness and forgetfulness. Then comes a phase of being lost and disconnected.

When you are in the grip of your sexual desires, your mind and body are being manipulated without your knowledge. Your basic logic, reasoning, and understanding of life are all pushed aside, and something else takes over. Your actions are not voluntary. They are not conscious. They are just happening. And then, once you reach orgasm and the energy that was holding you up drops you, you feel a sense of disconnection and loneliness. That is the sting.

There is no way to escape the stinging sensation of a sexual desire, because it is not meant to take you somewhere and keep you there. Eventually, it will push you down, and you will have to come back to a state that is much lower than where you started.

That is the very nature of any force that takes you deeper into unconsciousness. The further it takes you into unconsciousness, the more it will drop you down when it lets go. That is the very nature of how the mind works. With the same intensity with which you experience the peaks of sexual passion, you are also inevitably pushed to the deep dark corners where you have to start searching for yourself again.

That is why there is always a feeling of incompleteness after your chasing. You don't feel elevated. You don't feel liberated. You don't feel enlightened. You know you have experienced something here, something you want to experience again immediately, but your body does not have the energy to experience it again immediately, at least for a man. He has to wait. He has to replenish his energies. And then again, he has to do the same chasing, the same running. There is no way for him to consciously move towards it.

That is why no matter how satisfying your pursuit of a sexual desire might seem to be, at the end of it, it will leave you empty and hollow. And at the same time, you cannot suppress this desire. You cannot run away from this desire. Where will you hide? If you go underwater, that is when you can escape the stings of the hornet. But the moment your head comes up to take a breath, the stinging starts again.

He is using a beautiful analogy of water and hornets to explain how there is something within us. If we are able to drown ourselves in it, if we are able to drink that something that is all around us, we become immune to the pangs of sexual cravings. He is talking about a real experience that can help you transcend sex. Not by denying it, not by running away from it, but by fully becoming it.

The water he's talking about is consciousness, aliveness. As of now, you are away from the water. You are exposed. You cannot escape the stinging. Wherever you go, you will be chased. There are innumerable things - even seemingly unrelated things that have nothing whatsoever to do with sex - that will remind you of sex. Because the desire is there, because you know there is a pleasurable experience waiting at the end, you will find reasons to remind yourself.

In fact, the entire human society is arranged and organized in such a way that you can never fully forget sex. Sex is the very fabric on which the social structure is woven. What we see on the surface are images, experiences, but if you dig a little deeper and inquire into the nature of the fabric that is supporting those images, that is creating those experiences, you will find sex there.

Man has tried to hide this ultimate desire, his greatest of desires, by becoming busy, by diverting his attention away from it. If he does not stay busy all day, he'll only be thinking about sex. Leave a man to himself without meditativeness, without mindfulness, without a deeper understanding of himself, just the conditioning of the world, but nothing important to do, he'll only be thinking about sex - because that is the basic necessity of the body. In a way, the basic necessity of the mind as well, because in sex, there is a way to momentarily erase the influence of the mind and the body on the spirit. You can touch a zone of purity, and that is what you're craving for.

As long as you are outside, there is no escaping the stinging sensation. There is no escaping the grip of sexual passion. But if you try to suppress it, it won't work. That is what he's referring to when he says that going under the water momentarily is, in a way, to try and suppress it. You want to escape the stings momentarily. But because it's only a suppression, it is only a matter of time before you have to come up to breathe, before you have to resume your normal routine activities of life. You cannot be in a state of suppression all the time because suppression requires effort. It requires action. It requires you to do something. You have to create artificial ideas and concepts to suppress something as fundamental to your being as sex.

You need great support from the external structure - hence, the religious scriptures. The way the scriptures are arranged and organized shows that enormous force has been used in the language - including threats - to suppress sex to the point of saying it is a sin. "Unless you go beyond it, unless you conquer it, you're going straight to hell." But this has not elevated Man above sex. It has only made him more susceptible to its forces. He's become more trapped. Why? Because suppression is simply shifting the energies from one corner of your being to another. You're not throwing it out. You have not understood it. You can only elevate yourself above something by understanding it. There is no other way to go beyond certain primal desires other than by understanding.

Now, in matters of sex, understanding has been suppressed because the ultimate understanding of sex conflicts with all religious beliefs. Sex is not just an activity of pleasure, it is a door through which you can transcend all the limitations of life. You can experience what religions have called "heaven," right here on earth.

Man figured out very early that sex is way too powerful. If it is just pleasure, there is no need to suppress it. There is no need to condemn it. There's no need to talk or think about it, and there's no need for sex to occupy such an important central place in human civilization. The whole society revolves around sex. Almost everything is a reflection of the strong desire for sex. Why? Because it is not just pleasure, it is actually a door. It can actually be the answer to the most important questions of all. Who are you? Where did you come from? What is birth? What is death? What happens to you after death? Are you just a body? Are you just a mind - or are you something more? All these questions, sex answers intuitively.

But the only problem is, by the time the answer settles in and becomes a part of you, you are thrown out of it because you did not earn the right to be there. You accidentally fell into it, just like any other animal. There was no conscious effort. There was no striving. There was no longing to understand sex. You did not study the scriptures. You did not decipher the text. You did not move into it consciously. So you've not put in any effort, and there was no longing.

Now how can existence reveal its biggest secret, its greatest secret, without even that much effort? If that was the case, all animals would have been enlightened. All they have to do is just have sex, and they would be liberated. You have to earn. As a human being, you have to earn the right to understand sex, because it is a pathway to liberation. Just like all the different ways through which you can awaken, sex is one other way. The discipline, the understanding, the effort that is required in all other methods is also required in sex.

In fact, sex has to become a meditation. You have to look at it as not another pleasure-seeking endeavor, but a way to understand two of the most fundamental forces shaping your life - your mind and body. Because your mind and body are absolutely turned inside out during sex, you don't understand it - because you're not watching. You are so involved in it that you don't see what's happening. It is stripping all your identity. Man gets down to the very basic animal level when he's having sex. You could be a king, a poet, the world's richest man, a saint, or a sinner. It doesn't matter. When you are in the grip of sex, you are just an animal. The only thing that makes it spiritual, makes it human, is your conscious involvement. And that is a spiritual process.

For most people, sex is not a spiritual process. It is just a release. It is just an unconscious gathering of energies, and you want to be a part of it. You don't even know why you're moving towards it. You're just being pushed towards it because it is not just a simple pleasure-seeking activity. It had to be suppressed by religion because the understanding of sex leads to the ultimate understanding of life, which totally nullifies religion. Because what is the purpose of religion? It is to answer these questions - What is life? Where did you come from? What is death? What's going to happen to your body after you die? These are the only questions we are unable to answer in our day-to-day activities of life, and that is why we turn to religion. Religions have accepted this authority - that they can supply these answers. Now what if you can find these answers for yourself through something like sex? Could it be that simple?

Here we are, building our temples, cathedrals, and churches, going through sermons and rigorous body modifications, enduring pain and suffering, all in an attempt to understand the meaning of life. But here, you are saying you can have pleasure and still reach the ultimate understanding of life. Sounds like an absolute insight. That is why sex was condemned - because it is not only a path, it is a joyful path. It is a celebratory path. It is a painless path. You don't have to deny the body or all its pleasures; just by understanding it, you can transcend the desires. Just by understanding them, you can go beyond them.

That is what Rumi means when he says, "**You have to breathe the water.**" That means the water you're submerging in, that consciousness, that aliveness, should fill you up both inside and out. As of now, you're only becoming conscious once in a while. You are going to consciousness as a refuge only for a few moments every day. And then eventually, you have to come out of it because your dwelling is outside. You have created your dreams and desires, and the world of your dreams and desires is outside your conscious realm. So you have to step out of the water, and you cannot escape the stinging.

The only way to transcend sex is to drown yourself in your true being, drown yourself in your own consciousness. And that is what he means when he says, "You have to breathe the water." Once you can breathe the water and become one with it, there's no need to come out of it. The hornets will leave you alone.

No one looks for stars when the sun's out.
A person blended into God does not disappear.
He or she is just completely soaked in God's qualities.
Do you need a quote from the Quran?

Join those travelers.
The lamps we burn go out, some quickly.
Some last till daybreak.
Some are dim, some intense, all fed with fuel.

If a light goes out in one house,
that doesn't affect the next house.

This is the story of the animal soul,
not the divine soul.

The sun shines on every house.
When it goes down, all houses get dark.

"No one looks for stars when the sun's out." He's talking about an absolute merger of your individual animal soul with the divine soul. He's talking about union. Now when this union happens, it only appears like you have disappeared. Your ego is gone. Your mind is gone. Your body is gone. But only in theory. This sounds scary. This sounds disorienting.

But he gives a beautiful example: Where do the stars go during the day? You cannot see them because they have merged with the light of the sun - they haven't disappeared. They are still there. That is what enlightenment is. When you experience the transcendental nature of your being, you become one with it. When you become enlightened, you don't disappear. You become one with the ultimate. Your individual light merges with the divine light. You feel the oneness. You feel the completeness, but you can still recognize your mind. You can still recognize your body.

That is when you transcend your sexual passions and cravings. Why? Because there is nothing missing - you have become complete. That one moment of orgasm that was driving you crazy, that was pulling you towards it, has now become your whole reality. That single moment has expanded into eternity, and you have yearned to be there. By conscious effort, by expanding your awareness, by watching your body, by watching your mind, you have eventually merged your individual identity with the supreme identity.

Because there is no separation, there is no craving, and because you have moved consciously into experiencing the ultimate union, you know how to come back. You know what the terrain looks like. You know the signposts. You know the pitfalls. That is why next time when you navigate, you have a choice to be there for as long as you want. There is nobody throwing you out because you have earned your right to be there. What was your right? Consciousness. You were not blindfolded when you were thrown into that ecstatic space. You were wide awake. You walked through those gates with full awareness of what you're doing.

Yes, it is a scary experience because you know just beyond those gates, the merger, the union might be so complete, so spectacular that you might never want to come back to being yourself. That is the biggest fear in enlightenment - losing yourself completely. You're not afraid of going into sex because you're not allowed to be there for more than a single moment, then you are thrown out. Now what if you could stay there longer? Would you make a conscious decision to come back? Why would you come back?

When you have touched the ultimate, when you have become the ultimate, when you have breathed the water in and you have merged with the water, and when you know the hornets cannot come anywhere near you, why would you decide to come back again? That is the fear. And that fear is only because you have not experienced it. When you experience enlightenment, you will see as much as there is joy in becoming one with existence, there is also great joy in identifying yourself as the individual.

You would enjoy playing the game of life, because there are some things only the mind and body can do. While it is a play - it has no purpose, no meaning - as you have already attained the ultimate. Still, the game itself is enticing, but something will pull you back to the body. However, you won't come back as an individual - you will return as someone who is aware of the ultimate nature of your being. You will come back as someone who knows that they are not the body, someone who knows that they are not the mind. That is the kind of merging that you have to long for.

The Whirling Dervish

YOU ARE THE UNIVERSE

Join those travelers,
the lamps we burn go out, some quickly,
Some last till daybreak.
Some are dim, some intense, all fed with fuel.

If a light goes out in one house, it does not affect the next house. This is the story of the animal soul, not the divine soul.

The sun shines on every house, and when it goes down, all houses get dark.

Rumi is talking about the body as a burning lamp. It needs fuel. Some people live longer, while others have shorter lives. But we are all travelers on this journey, moving towards our true destination, our ultimate reality.

Our individual identity is limited. When you die, your body dies and your mind dies. Your light is limited to the house that it illuminates. If your light goes out, it does not affect the light of another house. This is your individual identity.

But once you become the sun, once you realize the ultimate nature of your being, then you will be the light that is shining through every house. This is a very deep philosophical understanding of life that Rumi is talking about. It is so deep that it is likely that you will miss it altogether. But let me try to put it into words - see if you can connect with any part of it.

What Rumi is saying is that as long as your identity is limited to the body and you are living as an individual animal soul, your birth and death are only your concern. They have nothing to do with what is happening outside. There is an independent objective reality outside where there are other people carrying their own lamps and going through their own journeys.

But once you realize the ultimate nature of your being, once you become the sun, you will know that when your light goes out, the light of the universe goes out. When you stop dreaming, the whole universe stops dreaming. When you stop seeing, everything stops seeing. This is the hardest thing to understand.

For an awakened individual, for an enlightened individual, he knows that when he finally withdraws himself from the world and consciously chooses to end his life, consciously chooses to leave the body and merge into the ultimate, he knows that he is withdrawing all the energies that he was using to create his reality.

That is why for the one who is awakened, his death is the death of one whole universe. It is not just the death of an individual. This is impossible to understand intellectually. Conceptually, it sounds ludicrous - it sounds nonsensical. But if you want to know what that feels like, what it feels like to be that light that is shining on everything, to see life as something that is emanating from the center that belongs to you, you have to become enlightened. You have to become awakened. Only then will you know that your universe, your world of dreams, was all your making. It was a part of your dream.

As long as you are identified with the limited body, you will always see other things. For you, reality will always be objective on the outside. And when you die, you will feel a sense that 'Only I am dying, the world will go on.'

But an enlightened man has no fear. This does not scare him at all because he knows that when he goes, his entire dreaming process goes away. He has realized the oneness of life. He has seen and experienced that there are no two things in existence. There is only one aliveness, one consciousness. And because he has realized this, for him, that is his consciousness. Of course, from the outside, when an enlightened person dies, for you, it is just a body dying. The world still goes on. You are still alive. You cannot understand this from the outside. But from the inside, nothing goes on. It is the complete withdrawal.

This is what is mentioned in religious scriptures as the end of the world. God breathes life and takes it away. This is the actual meaning. There is no God. There is no entity like God. It is just an individual who has realized the ultimate truth. His language would be something like this: "When I go, I take everything with me." He takes his world with him. Everything disappears. There is not a single religion that has not used such language: the end of the world. Because where do these scriptures come from? Ultimately, they come from one source, which is a man who has realized the ultimate truth.

That is why in the Gita, Krishna says, "I will come back every time there is unlawfulness. There is injustice. I will come to save the world." What does this mean? He is just saying that someone like him will take birth, someone who will realize the true nature of his being. One among you will awaken to the ultimate reality. And he will guide you on the path to liberation. That is the end of suffering.

It is not a god sending a messenger to liberate human beings. It is not that literal. It is an individual taking birth normally, just like everybody else, and growing in realization, growing in understanding. And once he awakens to his highest nature, he becomes the source of guidance, just like Buddha was, just like Jesus was.

Because we do not understand this process and we are so far removed from the simplicity of it, we create all kinds of religious concepts and worship those individuals as the only possibilities of the ultimate. In reality, they all spoke about that possibility existing within each and every human being.

Light is the image of your teacher.
Your enemies love the dark.

A spider weaves a web over a light.
Out of himself or herself makes a veil.

Don't try to control a wild horse by grabbing its leg.
Take hold of the neck. Use a bridle.

Be sensible, then ride. There is a need for self denial.
Don't be contemptuous of old obediences.
They help.

Rumi is saying that you do not have to fight your desires. You do not have to deny the body or the pleasures. Instead, you should approach them artfully.

You know this wild horse needs to be tamed but you cannot just grab hold of its leg, or it will kick you and hurt you. You have to understand it and tame it consciously, taking your time.

The wild horse that Rumi is referring to is your own passions, your mind, and your body. Once you know how to tame the horse, then you can ride it. Then it will be under your control. This is when you will see the true image of who you are, beyond the reflections. Only when you are able to sit on that horse, when it is in your control and you are riding it, will your self become the true image. Now, wherever you go, you are going. Before that, you were chasing the horse. You were tied to it, tied to your passions. So you were only lost in your self-reflections, ideas about yourself. But when you are able to understand your desires, you can see who you truly are.

Nazruddin was staring at a broken mirror frowning and shaking his head. A friend, passing by, asked, "What's the matter, Mullah?" Nazruddin replied, "I have been looking into this mirror for days, and it still won't show me the face I want."

Life is a broken mirror. At best, we can see only bits and pieces of ourselves. It is a fragmented, disconnected reality. Trying to find your true image in the world of experiences is like staring into a broken mirror. You will only see distorted, shattered, disconnected parts of yourself. Yes, you can recognize yourself in bits and pieces, but that is not satisfying. You need a coherent image, and there is no way to fix that broken mirror. That is the nature of reality outside. The light has already split. The mirror is already broken. There is no need to piece it together.

There is another mirror. An internal mirror, purer and more eternal than the external one. Stare into that mirror to know who you truly are.

THE SUFI

A Sufi was wandering the world.
One night, he came as a guest to a community of
Sufis.
He tied up his donkey in the stable
and then was welcomed to the head of the dais.
They went into deep meditation and mystical
communion, he and these friends. For such people,
a person's presence is more to learn from
than a book. A Sufi's book is not composed
with ink and alphabet. A scholar loves and lives on,
the marks of a pen. A Sufi loves footprints!
He sees those and stalks his game. At first, he sees
the clues. After a time, he can follow the scent.
To go guided by fragrance is a hundred times better
than following tracks. A person who is opening
to the divine is like a door to a Sufi.
What might appear a worthless stone
to others, to him is a pearl. You see your image
clearly in a mirror. A sheikh sees more than that
in a discarded brick.

A Sufi is a dervish who lives in the world, but he does
not belong to the world. If you were to meet a Sufi
during the routine activities of your life, if you just
happen to see him and interact with him, and if you

didn't know that he was a Sufi, you would not know how to recognize him.

On the outside, Sufis are just normal people. In fact, more ordinary than ordinary people. It is almost impossible to recognize them from the outside. It is said that only a Sufi can recognize a Sufi, because what they're looking for in people is something totally different. What a Sufi is looking for in another individual, in another Sufi, is something totally different from what a worldly man is looking for.

The worldly man is looking for information. He's looking for knowledge. He is seeing through his mind. He's looking for familiarity. He's looking for a structured framework of understanding. And we can see this when two people interact - more often than not, it's a conversation between two ideas, two ways of thinking.

But a Sufi does not belong to the realm of thinking. He has settled deeper. He has learned how to recognize another person. He has learned how to see from outside the confines of his mind. He has other faculties of seeing - he can smell things. He can intuitively feel things. Rumi says, "**A Sufi rather follows the scent than the footprints.**" A worldly man is not even looking for the footprints - he is in the world of books. He's in the world of knowledge.

Rumi's definition of a book is just a conceptual, theoretical understanding of life.

Sufis love to learn from another person. If given a choice between a book and a conversation with another Sufi, any day, he'd prefer a conversation with another Sufi. Because he has learned how to learn non-intellectually, how to assimilate knowledge, how to assimilate wisdom without bringing his mind - one conversation with a Sufi is equivalent to reading a hundred books.

If you look at the spiritual tradition, learning from books is a very modern phenomenon. There was a time when passing down spiritual wisdom was almost entirely oral. Rumi is talking about a sheikh. A sheikh is a teacher. Sufis refer to their masters, to their teachers as sheikhs. He is talking about the direct experience of truth, direct exchange of understanding of truth between a disciple and a teacher, and how, to a Sufi, that is so much more valuable than reading books.

The whole idea that an individual can walk the path of self-realization and attain to enlightenment on his own, is totally modern. For a very long time, spirituality has been an oral tradition. The conversations were not even recorded. If a student wanted to learn, he had to go to a teacher to get that direct interaction between a disciple and a master - where a student can watch and learn, can listen and learn, where a teacher doesn't teach but guides - he inspires.

More than what the teacher is saying, what he is, is what resonates at a deeper level within a student. There is something intangible, something real that you can feel when you're in the presence of a teacher. You cannot get that when you're reading a book. The words are the same. If you are adept at deciphering spiritual words, you can even get to the exact meaning. But one very important ingredient is missing: That is the depth from which these words are resonating, the intensity with which these words are being communicated, and how each word, each sentence, each understanding is wrapped in love.

You cannot capture all this in books. That is why when you read a master's words, it takes something more from you - your ability to add something more to that experience, to hold on to the practice. You have to bring love, connection, and reverence from inside. It is very hard to simply rely on words and go all the way to awakening - it is nearly impossible unless the student has already been introduced to the idea of what the relationship between a master and a disciple is. He should have come from a tradition, a culture where there is an unspoken reverence, love, and connection in that relationship. Either he's introduced to that idea very early as a part of growing up, or he has subconsciously accepted that "when I am reading the words of an enlightened master, I don't read it like any other words. I don't read it like any other book. For me, these words mean something more than what I am understanding."

There is always something more. You should be able to see the pain and struggle of the teacher to try and communicate something that he actually cannot communicate. You should be able to see the longing in the teacher's words. That is what Rumi is talking about. He is talking about the teacher. And he says, "You can see your face clearly in a mirror. A sheikh can see a thousand times more on a piece of brick." He's talking about the level of intelligence, the level of awareness of the teacher.

Sufi teachers are unique in a way that they will use anything and everything that is available around them and within them to teach. They are those rare individuals who have transcended the limitation of human ideas such as religion and belief systems. So if you are listening to a Sufi, he quotes from the Bible, he quotes from the Quran, he talks about Jesus, he talks about Mohammed. He has no restriction in terms of what to use to communicate that truth. This is one unique aspect of Sufism. Sufism is a mystical branch of Islam, but it is an amalgamation of all the different cultures of the world where a Sufi has understood the central core essence of different religions, different belief systems. So it doesn't matter what your religious background is, a Sufi can be your teacher.

The word Sufi is very beautiful. Etymologically, it has two meanings. It comes from the root word, 'suf', which means wool. Sufis wore simple ragged, woolen clothes as a symbol of their renunciation of the world - that is how a Sufi master is recognized. He always wears simple, recognizable, woolen clothes. Another meaning comes from the Arabic root 'saf,' which means pure. A Sufi is someone who has purified himself, purified his heart, and has experienced limitless love - that is what he teaches.

In fact, the word 'teaching' does not apply as well to a Sufi when compared to 'guiding', 'inspiring', 'illuminating'. To be in the presence of a Sufi master is a phenomenon by itself because you can see love in human form.

A Sufi master is someone who has transcended his ego. He is able to communicate between that ultimate truth and you without any interference of the ego. That is why he has no fear. He has no restrictions. He has no limitations. And even when he's not teaching, he's always communicating the essence of the truth that he has become.

So, more often than not, if you are around a Sufi teacher, it is hard to distinguish a teaching session from a normal conversation - the conversation itself is the teaching. Many times he could be talking about the food he's eating, he could be talking about the house he's living in, he could be talking about something very mundane, ordinary, very worldly - and yet his interpretation, the way he looks at something is how he teaches. He teaches without teaching.

Sufi masters are those
whose spirits existed before the world.
Before the body, they lived many lifetimes.

Before seeds went into the ground, they harvested wheat.
Before there was an ocean, they strung pearls.

While the great meeting was going on about bringing human beings into existence, they stood up to their chins
in wisdom water. When some of the angels opposed creation, the Sufi sheikhs laughed and clapped among themselves.

Before materiality, they knew
what it was like to be trapped inside matter.
Before there was a night sky, they saw Saturn.

Before wheat grains, they tasted bread.
With no mind they thought.

This transcends our limited understanding of what a human being is and what he is capable of. Rumi is not just talking about clairvoyance. He's not just saying that a sheikh, a Sufi master, has the ability to look into the future or has the ability to go to the past. He's saying a Sufi Master existed before all the things that he's talking about came into being.

This is not an exaggeration. This is not just a poetic way of showering praise on the teacher. There is something tangible, something real one can understand. A master is someone who has seen the transient nature of the mind and the body. He is someone who has experienced the purity of his own being, his own consciousness, his own awareness.

When you are given access to that pristine space very few people can enter, you are given access to the ultimate secret of the universe - the secret of how things are created, the secret of creation itself. That is why in awakening, in enlightenment, you don't just understand you. You don't just understand your limited mind or your limited body. You understand the whole universe. You understand the very process of creation.

And because you're at the very source of creation, you can see how everything you are experiencing has come about by your own interaction with the world. There was no world before consciousness. There cannot be matter before someone being there to perceive matter. There cannot be experiences before someone being there to experience things. He's talking about that one single ultimate reality that gives birth to everything else.

Everything that you can see and observe in the outside world - for the limited you, for your limited mind and body - appears to be outside. It seems like there is some other higher entity above and beyond your understanding that has created the world, including you. That is the understanding in which most human beings live and die. That is what they believe in. "There is something above and beyond me. I don't know what that is. So let me try and understand as much as possible of what's happening within me, what's happening outside of me, and eventually die one day." But an individual who has transcended the limitations of the mind and body, who has experienced the ultimate reality, cannot see creation as something separate from him. While this is so obvious in meaning, it is extraordinarily difficult to understand.

We know that enlightenment is a moment when you experience your own pure being and you're not experiencing your mind and body. If you're experiencing your mind and body, then it is just another experience. In fact, in your wakeful consciousness throughout the day, you are only experiencing your mind and body - the projections of your mind and the sensations of your body.

Enlightenment, by its very definition, means you have transcended all experiences. There is nothing to experience. There's no body. There's no mind. And yet you are there. What does that mean? That means you have become the primordial entity from which everything sprung into life. By definition, you are at the very source of creation. That is what Rumi is talking about.

Sufi masters have existed long before all things. He says, "**Before the body, they lived many lifetimes.**" Because he's not the body. It is only in this lifetime he is associating himself with the body. But as an enlightened being, he's above and beyond the body.

Before seeds went into the ground, they harvested wheat.
Before there was an ocean, they strung pearls.

While the great meeting was going on about bringing
human beings into existence, they stood up to their
chins
in wisdom water. When some of the angels opposed
creation, the Sufi sheikhs laughed and clapped
among themselves.

He's talking about how an awakened master is above
and beyond all experiences. That is why if you look at
the language religion uses, every religion believes that
creation started after the words were spoken - after
the words of their teacher were spoken.

For example, in Christianity - more importantly,
Judaism, the creation and the whole story of Adam
and Eve, is basically a story of enlightenment, a story
of awakening - two individuals, in the Garden of
Eden. The Garden of Eden is nothing but life. Life is
pure, pristine, beautiful, bountiful - that is what the
Garden of Eden is. These two individuals became
aware of themselves - that is awakening. When an
individual realizes the true nature of his being, that is
what awakening or enlightenment is.

Basically, the whole story of Adam and Eve is not the
story of creation but the story of enlightenment. And
yet, why does Judaism remember this story as a story
of creation? When an individual awakens to his
highest nature, he becomes the starting point of
creation because he can see, from his point of view

subjectively, that his whole life has been a part of his dreaming.

Subjectively, creation is a totally different experience when compared to observing it from the outside objectively. Most human experiences observe things from outside. You don't see the tree inside you. You don't see the birds inside you. You don't see the sky inside you. They're all outside. Because they're outside, there is no way to come to this understanding that, "I am a part of this creative process. I am responsible for that tree to be there." It almost sounds nonsensical. "How can I create that tree? How can I create the sky? I'm just a tiny body. I'm just a tiny creature. I'm just one of the creatures like everybody else."

That's because you are seeing yourself as a limited body, as a limited mind. That is why awakening is not a simple realization intellectually that "I am everything." It is an actual experience where you realize the totality of everything. When you have transcended the body, when you have transcended the mind, you have become the consciousness from which everything emerged. From that state, you can talk about the whole of creation as if it is coming from you.

That is why Jesus says, "I was before everything. I came before." His entire language is not only authoritative but also very subjective. He says, "You cannot reach God except through me. You cannot go to the Father without me. You have to pass through me." What does he mean? If he is just a body, if he is just a mind, why would he say something like that? It does not make any sense.

In the same tone, in the same breath, he says, "The Kingdom of Heaven is within you." Now if the Kingdom of Heaven is within you, why should you pass through him? There seems to be a great contradiction. The contradiction exists because of a lack of understanding of what he's talking about. When he says, "You have to pass through me," he's not referring to his body. He's not referring to him as an individual. He's referring to that consciousness, to that aliveness that he has become. He is referring to that oneness of life that permeates everything.

Human beings are living, swimming, and moving in the ocean of aliveness, the ocean of consciousness. They just don't see it. A Sufi master has become that ocean. Because he has become that ocean, he can see everything as an extension of his being, as an extension of that same energy.

The Whirling Dervish

THE FOURTH DIMENSION

Immediate intuition to Sufis is the simplest act of
consciousness, what to others would be epiphany.
Much of our thought is of the past, or the future.
They're free of those.
Before a mine is dug, they judge coins.
Before vineyards, they know the excitements to
come.
In July, they feel December.
In unbroken sunlight, they find shade.
In fana, the state where all objects dissolve,
they recognize objects.
The open sky drinks from their circling cup.
The sun wears the gold of their generosity.

Existence is a deep mystery. It is not linear. It is not
constructed the way the human mind sees it. For the
human mind, life is a movement from the past to the
future. It does not know the present. So every time it
reflects on the nature of experiences, invariably, it
either has to go to the past or the future. Because it is
not in the present moment, it is hidden and covered
up from all the mysteries of life.

Because it cannot be in the present moment, it cannot
see the simplest of things - that present is the only

reality. If the present is the only reality, then there is absolutely no contradiction when Rumi says, "A Sufi Master precedes all experiences." He was there before anything. He was there before the seed was sown in the ground, before the wheat was harvested. Because there is only the present moment, the present moment knows neither before nor after. If you can fully be in the present moment, then you would be a witness to everything that has ever happened because all things have to pass through the present moment. In fact, there is not even a passing. This whole idea of something moving from the past to the future is purely a mental construct.

Scientists say that there is no such thing called time. Time is simply another dimension in space. Einstein said this, and it was an absolute revelation when he said it. "We are living in a three-dimensional world moving through a fourth dimension we call time." In a way, he's right. He's saying time is simply a space that we cannot experience. Because we are limited, we are trapped in this three dimensional world, we have to wait to experience the movement of time.

The simplest way to understand this is to imagine if you are standing on the ground, you're staring ahead, and there is a curved road. There is a car moving along the road, but you cannot see it. For you, while you're standing there and staring, that car is somewhere in your future. If that car is actually moving on the road, you have to wait for that experience to become a reality for you. You don't know the existence of the car. It is somewhere in the future.

But imagine if there's a tree there, and if you happen to climb up that tree and then look ahead. Now you can see more of the road, and you can see that car far away. Just by shifting your position, the car that was in the future became your present. Time is exactly that. All that we will be experiencing in the future, in a way, is already there as a physical landscape somewhere because existence knows no past, no future - it only knows the present. If it only knows the present, then your entire future is already a part of the present.

You are stuck in the body, and you have to wait for tomorrow to experience whatever that's going to happen tomorrow. But if you happen to climb that tree of a higher dimension, if that tree were to extend into a higher dimension, a fourth dimension, you could see your future. You could see your past.

That is what meditation is. When you descend to the depths of meditation, you are actually going inside a fourth dimension. The very space you are occupying expands. That is why, initially, when you are trying to learn meditation, trying to understand what's happening , it seems very chaotic, confusing, and also painful because the space that is available for you to move around is very limited - you're stuck in the body. You're stuck in the mind. And the only space you can move around in, you're not supposed to move around in because that's what meditation is. You want to move around in the three-dimensional space, but that would take you out of meditation. So you have restricted yourself and that restriction is what feels like effort in meditation.

But after a while, there would be no effort in sitting in meditation. This is something that cannot be understood. Only someone who has gone deep enough knows that after a while, sitting in meditation is no effort. In fact, it's pure joy. It automatically draws you in. It is very relaxing to sit in meditation. Why? Because the space is expanding. Now, how can space expand when your body is just the same? Your mind is just the same? When you open your eyes and look at your body, your body has not expanded. In your three-dimensional world, your house has not expanded. The place where you're sitting in meditation has not expanded - everything is the same. Yet, you feel so much more space inside. Space has been added to your being. For the first time, you are becoming aware of an unknown dimension - an unknown space.

What does this mean? This space cannot be the regular three-dimensional space because somebody can be looking at you meditating and they will see no changes. There is no expansion. There is no relaxation. They are only seeing another human being sitting there.

The expansion is not happening in this three-dimensional space. It's happening in the fourth dimension. The fourth dimension, what we call time, is nothing but space. When you experience this, that is when you will know it is limitless. Unlike this three-dimensional space, in the fourth dimension you can go as far as you want. There is absolutely no limit to how far you can go in this universe. There are no walls. There are no edges where you can fall off. If you decide to go, you can keep on going. There's no end to it.

The fourth dimension is the present moment, and it is limitless. You can be in the present moment for as long as you want. And eventually, when you reach samadhi, the mahasamadhi, where you drop the body consciousness and you become one with the universe, you have become a part of the eternal present. A Sufi master is someone who has come from that space. Of course, to you, he is just a normal human being - same mind, same body. But he has access to that space which transcends all linear understanding of life.

That is why Rumi says,

Much of our thought is of the past or the future. They are free of those.
A Sufi master is above the past and the future; he dwells in the present.

Before a mine is dug, they judge coins.
Before vineyards, they know the excitements to come.

In July, they feel December.
In unbroken sunlight, they find shade.

It's a beautiful poetic way of saying that he is not waiting for an experience to happen to find joy, contentment and excitement. The very space he occupies, the present moment, contains all that he's looking for. There is no waiting for an experience. The experience is just a play. The present moment itself is the completion.

In unbroken sunlight, they find shade.
In fana, the state where all objects dissolve, they recognize objects.

'Fana' is a beautiful word. Fana is total annihilation. Absolute surrender. Fana is that moment where you completely lose yourself. Fana is an equivalent word for Nirvana, total transcendence. In the state of fana, there are no objects. There are no things to experience. There is only the experiencer. There is only the pure being that is experiencing. And here, Rumi says, even in that space, even in that experience of fana, when there are no objects, a Sufi master can see objects. It's a poetic way of saying there is nothing a Sufi master cannot see and experience.

The open sky drinks from their circling cup.
The sun wears the gold of their generosity.

He's saying that even seemingly inanimate, lifeless, physical things extend from the being. Everything is rooted in the experience of the being. Someday, if we are able to objectively come to this understanding, if science is able to discover - through some miraculous means - the existence of consciousness, it would have to go back and rewrite all the textbooks of science, all the textbooks of human knowledge. Every single concept, every single idea will have to be rewritten because we have missed the most important thing which occupies almost ninety percent of everything we are experiencing.

Everywhere you go, everywhere you see, in all dimensions, aliveness is filling the universe. Without taking into account the existence of that aliveness, the existence of that consciousness, all our theories and concepts are stupid, dull, and meaningless. As of now, we hold on to those concepts because they are useful - the language we use to describe those experiences helps us to connect one thing to another. It helps us to remember things. It helps us to use things.

If you were to study electricity, you are not actually studying electricity. You are studying the language of electricity that human beings have used. You are basically studying the concepts and theories the human mind has created to understand electricity. Existentially, it is total nonsense. Existence will simply laugh at that and say, "that's not how electricity works." But for a student who is studying it, it makes sense because he can use it. The true value of science is in its application. But the actual science, science that can illuminate the nature of reality, that can take into account the existence of aliveness, the existence of consciousness, will look at things very differently. All our concepts, ideas, and theories would mean nothing.

That is why when he says, "**The open sky drinks from their circling cup,**" for a scientific mind, for a logical mind, for a reasoning mind, that seems totally nonsensical. He's drunk. He's just lost in his teacher's words, and his teacher has mesmerized him. And he's saying, "**the open sky drinks from their circling cup. The sun wears the gold of their generosity.**" What nonsense. Where is the sun? And where is a Sufi master? The sun is the sun. It illuminates everything. Without the sun, nothing can exist. Everything can exist by itself without a Sufi Master. He's just one other human being.

We can say this because we don't know what it is to be at the center of creation. We don't know what it is to be at the center of life. We are only talking about concepts and ideas. For the one who has experienced the truth of life, the essence of life, he can see that there are no things. There are no objects.

Nazruddin was seen climbing up and down a ladder, repeatedly going from the ground to the roof of his house. A neighbor asked, "Mullah, what are you doing?" Nazruddin replied, "I heard that the secret to finding something is to start looking from the top down. So I'm checking the roof first."

Now, that is the story of religions. They have words but they don't know it's all inner. These words don't mean anything in the outer world. And they are nowhere near the inner. They have used these words to create an outer world away from our present reality and they have literalized the concept of heaven and hell, and the whole idea of the migration of the soul and the experience of the truth, the judgment of the soul - all that happens inside an individual. They have taken a spiritual concept literally. That is why religions don't make any sense. You have to be blind. You have to stop asking questions. You have to stop seeking to be able to accept the beliefs of a religion.

That is why there have always existed lesser known mystical branches dedicated to the exploration of truth hidden within every mainstream religion. Sufism in Islam, Gnosticism in Christianity, and the Vedantas in Hinduism. Almost every major religion has a tiny branch somewhere which tries to stay as far away from the main religion as possible - because the central essence is there, the words are there, but only these mystical branches, the teachers of these mystical branches, know how to interpret the words of their religion.

So if you really want to understand what your religion is teaching you, if you cannot drop it, then there is no other way but to understand it. And the way to understand it is to go to a Sufi master. Go to a mystical teacher. If there is an opportunity to be with a teacher, to listen to his words directly, to bathe in the experience of his love, that should be more preferable than just sitting and reading his words.

TEAR DOWN THIS HOUSE

Tear down
this house. A hundred thousand new houses
can be built from the transparent yellow carnelian

buried beneath it, and the only way to get to that
is to do the work of demolishing and then

digging under the foundations. With that value
in hand all the new construction will be done

without effort. And anyway, sooner or later, this house
will fall on its own. The jewel treasure will be

uncovered, but it won't be yours then. The buried
wealth is your pay for doing the demolition.

Rumi is talking about a house, and he's urging you to demolish the house. What is he talking about? And he says there is a treasure buried underneath. All you have to do is dig. He's talking about the body. The treasure he's talking about is the self. Body is the house he wants you to destroy. He says that sooner or later, whether you want it or not, the body will be destroyed. It is the nature of the body to eventually return to the source. It has no reality of its own - it is an imaginary construction. It is existing because you want it to exist. It is existing by the force of your own will, your desires, the desire to accomplish those desires, and your desire to use the body to accomplish those desires. There is some pleasure-seeking going on that feels real.

You have figured out a way of experiencing momentary pleasures of life, and you've also figured out that your body can help you experience those pleasures. So, you want the body. But the body by itself has no desire to be - it is constantly trying to return to the source. If you don't pay enough attention to the body, if you don't take care of it, if you don't nourish it, it will destruct itself. The body is a self-destructing mechanism. It is all the while looking for ways to disappear, but you want it to be alive, so you keep it alive. You nurture it, you care for it, you drag it along for years, while you can see that it's becoming harder and harder. You are fighting with your body - you can see that. The more attention you give it, the more attention it needs. The body is a mysterious phenomenon. It needs constant repairing, constant work. It's like a house that is falling apart.

Rumi says to start digging before this house is demolished. Because if you dig, the treasure is yours. For the work that you will be putting in, the reward is the treasure buried underneath it. But if you don't dig, if the house falls by itself, then you will regret because the treasure won't be yours. He is talking about something deep. While he's using the analogy of a house and the treasure, he's actually talking about something very existential, also very scientific. He's using the words carefully. He's talking about death. He's talking about rebirth. He's talking about reincarnation. He's talking about awakening in very precise terms. But because he's a poet, he's able to talk about such a deep and complex subject in baby language. It is so easy to understand and also so easy to miss.

He's saying that whatever you are searching for in life, that is what has kept you alive, kept you going, and kept you awake. You are searching for something - that cannot be doubted. Your life is a search. But you are searching in the wrong place. You are searching where it can never be found, where it has never been found.

There are countless examples of individuals who have searched on the outside and have never found it. They have searched every which way possible. There is only one place where you can truly search. That is underneath your own house, beneath your own body. So he's saying you cannot go out, there is nothing out there. Your very house is standing on the treasure.

Your body is covering up the treasure. The treasure is actually not hidden - you are the one who's hiding it because you have built a house on top of the treasure in your unconsciousness, in your sleep, when there was not enough light. You built your house in the dark so you could not see the treasure.

Birth is deep unconsciousness, so you had no choice. It happened, and you quickly started building because that is what you saw all around you. Wherever you looked, there were people building their own houses. In fact, you lived in a world of houses. Your mother was a house. Your father was a house. They each had made it their life to build their house as well as they could. All they spoke about from morning until evening was about the house. What is the purpose of the house? How to take care of it. How to protect it, how to use it. All the conversations were about the house. And we can see that whenever you meet people, when you talk to them, they don't even realize they're only talking about the shell that is the body, but that is what they talk about all the time. There are no conversations about the self. There are no conversations about silence, about stillness. It's all about the body.

Because you saw only houses and you lived in the world of houses, you quickly started building your own. You didn't want to be left out. That was your process of learning, of accumulating knowledge, of growing up in the world. It was your body growing and acquiring the necessary skills and strengths. It was your house that was becoming stronger, more beautiful, and more livable - not you. You were not growing. Only your house was growing.

And then when you realized that you couldn't find what you're looking for in this house, you started going out. You started looking for answers on the outside. You could see that people were living in their houses, but just like you, they were always looking for something on the outside, because inside, the houses are dark and dimly lit. There are a lot of things hidden there, but you don't explore it. You don't look inside, because nobody talks about the inside of the house. Nobody cares about the inside of the house. Your entire conditioning is about the outside. How does it look to someone else? Your internal understanding of life is completely based on the external assessment of people around you.

So you started replacing your own intuitive understanding of life with explanations of life - what the voices from the outside were telling you: "I don't like the color of your windows." Oh, really? I need to change the color there. But I don't have paint, so I'll need to go and work for it. First, get the paint. Forget about everything else. Don't sit in the house idle.

Don't enjoy being in the house because the windows don't look good. So you go out into the world, searching for the paint, and then you realize this paint is not readily available. You have to get something else to get the paint. Everything has a price in the world, because everybody is looking for the same thing. Everybody is looking to beautify their houses, so there's a price put on everything.

Now you go into the world, searching for those simple colors, a little bit of wood, a few construction materials that can make your house beautiful, and then you realize you have to spend enormous amounts of time working on the outside away from your home to be able to satisfy those who are looking at the house from the outside.

But inside, you are perfectly fine with the house. It's giving you shelter. It's giving you comfort. Yes, it has some basic needs, and you know how to take care of it, but now your life has become something totally different from what it was supposed to be. It was meant to be an experience of being in the house. Now it's become an experience of trying to satisfy your idea of what an ideal house is. Your search took you away into the busy streets of life.

One day, Nazruddin was seen searching for something under a street light. A neighbor passing by asked, "What are you looking for, Mullah?" Nazruddin replied, "I lost my key." The neighbor asked, "Oh, did you drop it here?" Nazruddin answered, "No, I lost it in my house." Surprised, the neighbor asked, "Then why are you searching here?" Nazruddin replied, "Because there's more light here."

We're searching in the wrong place because our insides are unfamiliar to us. Because we have not illuminated the inside using the light of awareness, because we are living in a dark room, we don't like being there. We have illuminated the outside using artificial lights. And what is an artificial light? It is what we call intelligence. Intelligence is a tiny component of awareness. It can illuminate things only partially. By its very nature, intelligence is limited because it is passing through the filters of the mind and the body.

The awareness, the consciousness is pure. It's at the center. When it is being used by the mind and the body - because of the conditioning of the mind and the body, because of the limitations of the mind and the body - it becomes partially available. That is what we refer to as intelligence. We've illuminated the outside world using this limited intelligence. So when you look outside, you don't see pure awareness. You don't see pure consciousness. You don't see anything pure. You're only seeing your mental constructs. It is all creative. It looks intelligent, it looks sophisticated. "Look, there is a bridge. Look, there is a building."

You see the creations of the mind and the body - and the entire civilization is proud of all these creations. But what they don't understand is that these creations are simply limited intelligence. They are all passing away. They're all transient. They're all impermanent. But you're using them as if they are real, so you're being used by the intelligence of your own mind. It is not only your body that is controlling you, it is also your intelligence. That's why Rumi says, **"You wander around the world searching for the diamond mine when the real diamond mine is in your backyard."** The backyard is your own body. The diamond mine is the treasure that is buried within you.

Human beings have created many intelligent things, and you can travel, you can explore this world of human intelligence without realizing that the true intelligence, awareness, which is the totality of all that you are seeing on the outside, is hidden within you. That is the treasure Rumi is talking about. He's talking about a treasure that can reveal the true nature of who you are. It is the ultimate treasure. There cannot be a treasure more valuable than that. How can there be?

If you were told that there is something hidden right underneath you and that the moment you find it, you will know everything there is to know about you and the world around you, would you substitute that with knowledge? Would you substitute that experience for any other treasure? All other treasures are useless compared to the treasure that reveals the true nature of who you are, because that is what puts an end to your long, arduous, painful, human journey of searching. That is what puts an end to your suffering. There cannot be anything more valuable than that.

Rumi says it's not too far away. You don't have to go anywhere. You only have to recognize the world as illusionary. It is enticing. It draws your attention. But if you become aware of yourself, if you become rooted in the present moment and then look at the world, you will see that it is a mere projection through your mind. The projector is inside. It can show you as many worlds as you need. It can create innumerable worlds like the ones you're seeing on the outside with no effort. The source of it all is inside.

Tear down
this house. A hundred thousand new houses
can be built from the transparent yellow carnelian

buried beneath it, and the only way to get to that
is to do the work of demolishing and then

digging under the foundations.

Now, what is the work of demolishing he is talking about? He is talking about the destruction of the body, but the body is not really a physical thing to destroy. It is mainly a self-image that you have created for yourself. In fact, when you fall asleep, where is the body? When you close your eyes, notice how quickly your body diminishes to being a simple bundle of sensations. It's only when you have your eyes open that your body seems to be real - it seems to actually be there because everything you're seeing on the outside is a reflection of your body. The physical reality that you see is shaped by the inferences and interpretation of the body.

When you look at something solid, you know it is solid because your body has interacted with that. So in a way, in all your experiences on the outside, you are bringing your body. When you go to a new place, and when you're looking at something beautiful, you don't just look at it. You always put yourself in the middle of that experience - that is what takes you from one place to another. Because when you want to experience something, enjoy something, you immediately put your body there, although you're not seeing your body, you are seeing **through** the body. You are imagining that experience by putting the body in the middle of it. "Oh, it would be nice if my body were to experience this." That is the starting point of pleasure. You want to give that pleasure to the body. So you project it out there.

So whether you want it or not, when you keep your eyes open, you are always bringing the body into the picture - the subtle body, the self-image. Now that's what Rumi is talking about that needs to be destroyed. In a way, your self-image is your ego. The demolishing is the work of watching the ego. There is no way to destroy something illusionary, something imaginary, other than by illuminating it, other than by shedding light on it.

If your body were to be physical, if it were to be real, if it had its own reality, then there's no way you can destroy it by simply sitting and watching it. But Rumi says, "**The world is illusionary. A million other worlds can be created if you find that treasure.**" That treasure is aliveness, it is awareness, and that can manifest itself in as many ways as you want. Because physicality is not a reality, demolition happens simply by understanding it. Simply by breaking through the illusion. Simply by realizing that it is an illusion. That is why self is always a realization. It is not an experience. It is not an achievement. You just have to realize that your body isn't real.

The demolition work is the process of meditative watching and then digging under the foundations.

You have to go inward. You cannot go out. Digging is simply refusing to go out. If you stay inside and start brightening the lights of your house, one switch at a time, one corner at a time, if you start becoming more and more aware of what's happening inside, that will automatically take you deeper. That is the process of digging.

With that value
in hand all the new construction will be done

without effort. And anyway, sooner or later this house will fall on its own. The jewel treasure will be

uncovered, but it won't be yours then. The buried wealth is your pay for doing the demolition.

If you don't consciously demolish the house, then when that house gets demolished by itself - when death happens, when you reluctantly leave the body, when your body is snatched away from you - you will not be awake enough, aware enough to hold on to the treasure called you. It won't be yours. You might have to start digging again in your next life. You might not be reintroduced to that idea. You might be so lost again in another house, in a new construction, that you might not come back to digging.

You have to start digging now, in this lifetime, because already the clock is ticking against you. You don't have all the time in the world, because there's some intelligence that is already pushing the body towards its destruction. There is something wanting to go beyond the confines of the body. If you don't realize 'that something' consciously, you will not know that something is you. And if you don't know that, then you don't know you. The illumination has happened, the house is gone. But you're left with nothing. Your entire life would have been for nothing if you have only been living on the outside, searching for things that can beautify your house, and you've forgotten what is the purpose of the house. What is it hiding? Then when the house is demolished, you lose everything.

The pick and shovel work. If you wait and just
let it happen, you would bite your hand and say,

'I didn't do as I knew I should have.' This
is a rented house. You don't own the deed.

You have a lease, and you have set up a little shop,
where you barely make a living sewing patches

on torn clothing. Yet only a few feet underneath
are two veins, pure red and bright gold carnelian.

You don't own the house. You cannot hold on to it forever. You can beautify it as much as you want. You can decorate it as much as you want. You can make it into the most desirable house in the whole world, but it's not your house. You're living on a lease. That is the contract between you and existence. And there itself lies the biggest secret of the purpose of the body. It is to uncover the truth that it hides. Otherwise, there is no need for the body to be so ephemeral. It could have existed forever. There is no need for the body to constantly be needing your attention. There is no need for the body to constantly remind you that it's disappearing - it will eventually go away. This entire process is not needed, if not for the treasure that it's hiding.

Body is a leased property, because you are given that much time, that much space to start digging. But when you forget the true purpose of the body and start obsessing over the body, start clinging to the body, life becomes a frustrating experience because you have forgotten your contract. That is how people live their entire lives - they live as if they're going to be here forever. They live without contemplating death. They live only on one side of life, out of balance. They're only thinking about life. They're only thinking about living. They're only thinking about the body. They're only thinking about giving all the necessary comforts and luxuries for the body. And not only their bodies - as quickly as they can, they want to produce more bodies. They want to multiply.

The desire is there because your body is, somewhere deep down, losing that vitality. You want to see yourself younger again. You want to see yourself singing, laughing, and dancing again, you want to see that innocent part of you again. And the best way to see that is in your own children, because they look like you. They talk like you. They remind you of yourself. So you create more bodies, and then you start nurturing multiple bodies.

You came here to find out the truth of who you are. That is your ultimate purpose. That is why you were given a house. That is why you were given a limited contract and told - in this lifetime, this is your house, this is where the treasure is, and here is your pickaxe. The tools that are necessary for digging are already within you. You don't have to go find it outside. It's your own awareness. It's your own consciousness. Look at the beauty of existence. It puts you inside a house, it gives you the basic comforts, and it says, here are the tools to dig as well.

We forget that and we start obsessing over the body and creating more bodies, and that is where we get lost. And then, every time we are reminded of death, we feel uncertain. We feel fearful because we are never ready to go. We have never contemplated the inevitable, which is the most important part of the contract. The contract does not make any sense if not for its termination. The agreement between us and life makes sense only because that agreement will come to an end at some point in time. That is what death is.

And if you take away death, what is the meaning of this contract? There's no contract at all. The whole point of a contract is to actually say what will constitute the ending of the contract. That is why we create a contract. If the contract were to be eternal, then what is the necessity to create a contract? If you could just live in your body forever, and if you could possess it, if you could claim it, then there's no need to contemplate death. There's no need to start digging. There's no need to start searching.

It is because death is a part of the agreement. And you can never forget that because that is what gives all the meaning to the contract. That is what gives all the meaning to living. Because it is momentary, because it is transient, because it is slipping away, it reminds you of the true purpose of your being. Otherwise, you would never know that there is something hidden there, and you need to search for it.

Quick! Take the pickaxe and pry the foundation.
You've got to quit this seamstress work.

What does the patch sowing mean you ask. Eating
and drinking. The heavy cloak of the body
is always getting torn. You patch it with food,

and other restless ego satisfactions.

Rip up one board from the shop floor and look into the basement. You will see two glints in the dirt."
Eating and drinking are patchwork; that is the maintenance. And all the sense pleasures - he uses a beautiful word, ego pleasures. We are not even chasing after those things that the body truly needs - we are chasing after those things that we think the body needs. That is what the ego is. It is a collection of self-images, a collection of voices, a collection of interpretations of what that house is. And you're not only chasing after things that can help you repair the house, but you're also chasing after things that you think your house might need at some point in the future. You can see how easy it is to make your entire life into a purely mind and body phenomenon and forget yourself.

That is why it is so easy to live without asking the most important questions of life. Why am I here? Why do I even have a body? How can you live in peace without answering these questions? What are the questions you are asking? All other questions are useless if you don't answer this one question. Who are you? What is your purpose? Without answering these fundamental questions, even if you find answers to all your other questions, if you try to investigate into the nature of reality, if you go into a philosophical inquiry of what life is, a scientific inquiry or religious exploration of what life is - even if you were to find all the answers, it will be useless, because the only question that actually needs answering is, who are you?

But your attention has been conveniently diverted onto other things because you've been listening to those who have forgotten to ask this question about themselves. You've been living in a world of the blind, the deaf, and the mute. You've been living amongst those who have forgotten how to search, who have forgotten to ask the right questions. So all their inquiries, all their answers, while appearing to be useful, never address the fundamental question of who you are. That is why it is impossible to find answers if the question is not yours. That is the first thing to notice. Who is asking this question? Who introduced this question into my mind? Did my parents introduce this question? Did I pick up this question from my education sitting in those classrooms, listening to the teachers? Did I pick it up from somewhere outside? Is this really my question?

If you don't ask that question, if you start chasing after answers and if you're good at it, if you put in enormous effort, if you're intelligent enough, you will find the answers - because you are capable of finding answers. Now what happens when that day comes when you realize the question was not yours? And it has nothing to do with you. There cannot be a bigger regret than that. That is why most lives are forgettable lives. Most lives are pointless, meaningless lives. That is why most people die in utter disillusionment. They have not yet begun their conversation with life. They haven't even started their true interaction with life and their time's up.

Most people die filled with regrets - filled with regrets of all the things they should not have done. It's not the things that you did, but the things that you could not do, the things that you forgot to do - to be with yourself, to understand yourself, to stay close to yourself, to become meditative, to move towards self-realization. The day you get to know about self-realization and when you understand that there cannot be anything above that, the only regret you will have is not having heard about it sooner - not having the opportunity to start the search sooner. You will not be worried about the things you did not accomplish or about the dreams that you did not chase. The only regret you will have, is why didn't I start earlier?

So, the moment you start asking the right questions, the moment you get to your question, the question that is coming from inside you - ask that question forcefully, no matter how idiotic, no matter how silly it may seem to the world outside. Because they don't know you. They only know your house. But you are not the house. You are the one who's living in it. So your questions will be different. Your answers will be different. Your effort, your digging, your finding will be totally different from theirs.

The language of the world will always be different from the language of the self. The conversation between a spiritual being and a worldly being would be totally nonsensical. They both will be talking about something entirely different. But because there are so many living in the world of houses - living in a materialistic world, it is natural to feel lonely as a spiritual being. It is natural to doubt. "Why are the conversations in my head so different from the conversations in their heads?" Every individual who has asked the most important questions about himself, about herself, has felt this. "Maybe there's something wrong with me." But only those who have continued to ask despite not getting the support from the outside have found the answer.

And what is the answer? The greatest treasure you can find. Your own true being. An experience of the pure you without the disturbance of the mind, without the disturbance of the body. The answer to all the questions - What is the purpose of life? Who am I? Why did I come here? What is birth? What is death? What is the universe? All these questions will be answered in that moment when you realize the true nature of your being. And you don't have to go too far. See the house for what it is and start digging.

TRUE SELF

The minute I heard my first love story,
I started looking for you, not knowing
how blind that was.

Lovers don't finally meet somewhere.
They're in each other all along.

One of the hardest things to understand about searching for truth is how close you are to it, and yet how far. If you can only see that flimsy thing that is blocking the grandness, if you can see how easily the sun is hidden by the shadow of your thoughts, the day you break through the veil of thoughts and become the sun, you will realize how close you have always been, and you cannot help but laugh.

Searching for love, the quest for love, is the quest for the self. There is a natural longing to become one with it. That is why the search for yourself is not social, not religious - it is not added to you from the outside. You are born with it. This longing to become one with yourself is the primary force that has kept you alive, that has kept you going, that has kept you afloat in moments of despair, in moments of confusion. If not for this search, if not for this existential search that is inbuilt within you, you would have been so lost in the world of thoughts, in the world of ideas, it would have been impossible to even pause and ask the questions, "Who am I? What is the purpose of my life?"

The starting point of the search is always the acceptance of ignorance. "I don't know what I'm searching for. There is no way for me to know because I am not looking for another thing. I am looking for the oneness of life. I'm looking for something that cannot be divided. I'm looking for something that can complete me." How can such a thing be outside of me and give me the sense of completion? It's impossible.

If you are searching for something and if you find it, you should know that you have found something else. You have found something other than you because when you find yourself, there is no finding. There is no meeting. You cannot shake hands with yourself and say, "I have finally met you. Oh, this is how you look. Now I understand the nature of reality. Now I know what I was searching for." There is no scope for all this. In all this, there is still a separation.

But somewhere, there is also another inbuilt mechanism within us, which transforms anything real into an idea first. If you start searching for something, even before you start moving towards it, your mind presents you with a concept, a theory, an idea of it. True search begins only when you acknowledge what the mind is projecting and accept that it is not what you are searching for. It starts by knowing the difference between your mind and what you're searching for.

While you cannot speculate on the nature of that thing you're looking for - the nature of that experience - you can call it by many names, but you just don't know. At least you can be certain of what it's not, because all your experiences are happening through the mind. At least you can negate the false until you reach the true. That is the only thing that is in your control, that is in your understanding, that you can actually do. This is what separates a seeker who's thirsting for union and a seeker who's searching for justification.

If you're thirsting for truth, you will reject all experiences of the mind, the colors of the mind, the images of the mind, the sounds you hear. You know what a dream is. If you saw Jesus in your dream, if you saw Buddha in your dream, and if you convinced yourself, "This is what I was searching for. I was longing to meet my savior and here, I saw him. I actually saw him. He came to me. He spoke to me. He told me what I have to do." While you are having that experience, it is a real experience for you, just like any other experience that happens in a dream. So when you wake up in the morning - or if this has happened during your meditation, when you step out of your meditation - you might talk about this experience as if it's the ultimate experience - there cannot be anything above it. "What can I experience more than meeting Jesus or Buddha, or any other deity I'm worshiping?"

But that is where a seeker who's thirsting for union, who's searching for love, and the one who's just searching for a justification of what he's searching for get completely separated. The one who's longing will feel the separation, even when he's narrating that story, even when he's enthusiastically recollecting the experience, his heart is telling him that the union has not happened. He has only seen an image. He has not become what he's searching for. But the one who's just searching for an experience of the mind, who has not accepted his ignorance, will easily fall into the trap of believing that he has actually found the truth.

So, that's the difference between the one who is truly longing and the one who is sincerely searching, but the longing is missing. That is why spirituality is not just a search or a quest; it's a deep longing. Every part of your being, every cell in your body, should be screaming in pain because it is disconnected from the source. That longing should be so profound that there should be no way an image of something, an experience your mind is projecting, can substitute for the truth.

Why is this important to understand? Because there are a lot of people, innumerable examples of people who have turned inward looking for the answers of life, and they have found it in their own mental projections. They have substituted truth for their desires - their desire to meet a deity, their desire to experience truth in a certain way. If they saw a blinding light, if they saw the pearly gates of heaven, if they saw angels - anything you see is a part of your dreaming. Truth cannot be seen, and you cannot experience it. It is only in language, in words, that it is described as a search, a union, as consciousness, light - it's all in the world of language.

In real experience, there is no meeting possible. It is impossible for you to meet your lover. Rumi says, **"Lovers don't meet, they are in each other already."** Where is the separation? What has separated you from yourself? How can you be separated from yourself so much that you have to search for yourself? How can you long for yourself? You can do that only in ideas because something is blocking you from the pure perception of your being. That much is certain. You are experiencing yourself as something other than what you are, that much is certain. There is something more added to your pure experience of life.

You're taking a walk, but "you" are not walking. You are not just the walking. You are something more in that moment. You're sitting quietly, but "you" can't sit quietly. There is something more in that moment. There is something added to you. You're looking at a beautiful sunrise, but not able to enjoy it because there's something more in that moment - a conversation, an image, a judgment, a fear. That is what is blocking you from the pure perception of life.

Every moment you are already in deep communion with yourself. By the very definition of you, you cannot be separated from you. There cannot be two of you. How can there be one "you" searching for another "you"? At least we can be certain that what we are searching for is ourselves. It cannot be something outside us. If you're looking for something outside of you, something that you think is going to be different from you, totally alien to you, then you have not even begun your search. Then probably, you're searching through your religious scriptures because it is religions that put the search on the outside.

Spirituality is an internal search. Right from the beginning, you know that you're searching for a deeper experience of yourself, an unpolluted experience of yourself, a seamless experience of yourself. Now, what has happened to that experience? It has not disappeared. You're not missing it. You're not disconnected from it. You are experiencing everything through it, because there's "something more," and the nature of that "something more" is disturbance.

You are conditioned to recognize disturbance, to recognize movement, to recognize change, and even the smallest of disturbances. Actually, the disturbance is not that great. The separation between your true being and your muddled and confused being is very small. In fact, you will be amazed how small and how insignificant that disturbance is compared to the true nature of your being. There was actually nothing separating you from the seamless experience of your being. The only difference is that pure being is not disturbance. What is covering it is disturbance, and your mind is completely tuned towards recognizing disturbance.

It's like you walk into a dark room - it's pitch black, and there is one white spot somewhere in that room. On the black wall, there is one tiny spot. You can hardly recognize it, but it's there - a white spot. The darker the room, the easier it is to spot that white spot. Why? Because it provides a perfect contrast.

Now, what if you cannot recognize the color black? What if you are born partially blind and you cannot see black? You walk into that room. What is the first thing you see in that room? That white spot. That is the only thing that exists for you. Why? Because of two things. One is that the white spot is made visible because of the dark background. And the second thing is, you cannot see black. So that white spot is your reality. That's exactly how you are perceiving reality now.

You are living in an ocean of consciousness, aliveness. It is the black room. It is the very space you are in, the very space you are occupying. It's all around you, inside you, and outside you. It's everywhere, but it's utterly silent, totally non-disturbing. It is not trying to draw your attention in any way. It is only there as a presence. What you are experiencing as your presence is actually that presence. There is no "your presence." You are not alive. You know nothing about aliveness. Your body knows nothing about aliveness. Because it is swimming in this ocean of aliveness, it appears to be alive.

Your body is dead. Your mind is dead. They are purely mechanical, just patterns, random movements, energies that are stimulating you. There is no beingness there. There is no one sitting inside the body and perceiving it. There is someone outside of it, someone around it - who stretches all the way to the sky, who stretches all the way to the edge of the galaxy, who stretches all the way to the beginning of the universe, who stretches beyond everything known and unknown. That aliveness, that consciousness is the fundamental reality of existence.

Because it is the fundamental reality of existence, and you are at the center of it, you have no way of seeing it because you are it. And what is it that you are seeing? You are seeing that one small wave which you recognize as a thought, which is nothing but that white spot. Because that is what you are conditioned to recognize - you are tuned to recognizing disturbance.

For example, you're sitting and listening to me now. Basically, what am I creating to draw your attention? What am I doing? I am disturbing your peace. I am resonating in your consciousness. I am knocking at the doors of your being using my voice, using my actions. If I were to simply sit still, if I didn't speak, how long would you be able to sit there and look at me? You would either fall asleep or start taking a walk.

It's exactly the same thing that happens with the mind. When something is not moving, when something is absolutely still, you either fall asleep, you don't want to watch it, or you start drifting in thoughts - because you don't know what to do with it. That is the problem with what you're searching for. You don't know what to do with it. You don't know how to find it. You don't know that it is very close to you. And the disturbance that is blocking the pure consciousness is infinitesimally small.

That is why the day you are able to see the black instead of the white, you will laugh. How can you not laugh? Because what you were searching for was more abundant, was a million times more abundant, more obvious, than the disturbance you were attached to. Your mind, your body, all your thoughts, all your desires, this entire world will shrink to the size of a mustard seed. The whole universe would be nothing bigger than a grain of sand. You were so occupied, you were so attached to this grain of sand. You didn't know that there was pure space around it. You didn't know this grain of sand is actually on a beach. And that beach is a part of the ocean. You didn't know any of that. Your identity was completely locked on that grain of sand.

Now, what happens when you discover that you are the beach, you are the very ocean, and you have always been that. So how do you search for it? If you are a grain of sand, how do you search for the beach? Can you go somewhere and find it? Can you visualize the beach in your mind and find it? Can you meet your beach God in white robes and long flowing hair? Or matted hair and sandals? How? How can you find what you're looking for when you are already there? The beach is made of sand grains, and you are a sand grain. If sand grains are removed, then what is a beach?

You are the very thing you're searching for. The only difference is you are searching for the "you" that is not attached to the body, that is not attached to the mind - which is nothing but one single sand grain. You are the very beach. You are the very ocean. You are the very waving. Everything that is around that grain of sand belongs to you; that's your very space.

Even at this very moment, as you're listening to my voice, you are creating certain images in your mind. You're seeing a beach in your mind. You're seeing a sand grain in your mind. But where is all this happening? You are imagining vastness. How can it happen in your tiny head? No way. It is happening on the screen of your being, which is not limited to your body. That is because you are already the truth, and the disturbance that is covering the truth is so little, you don't feel trapped in the body, you don't actually want to break out of it. You are content being in the body. You're content being asleep.

How many people are waking up in the morning and are trying to go beyond their bodies? How many are saying, "I am trapped in this body, I want to escape this?" Not many. Why? Because they're actually not trapped. It is only in the idea that they are the body, they are trapped. Existentially, they are still the vastness that is supporting everything. That is why they can live in the body, think that they are nothing more than the body, and still go on living their lives as if they are something totally different.

Look at human beings. Theoretically, we accept that we are just a product of biological evolution, simply an extension of existence, and are just like any other animal. Theoretically, we look upon our bodies as nothing more than just another animal. But look at the activities of humans. Look at what has been created - music, poetry, literature, architecture, astronomy, recording of history, spirituality. Why? Why are these things even necessary for an animal? They aren't. You are not an animal. You are a pure being. You are a transcendental being.

You love literature, poetry, music, and dance because that's your nature. Joy is your nature. Bliss is your nature. You know nothing about death. You know nothing about birth. You have always been here. This is your realm. You cannot go anywhere else. This is where you belong. This is the only thing you know. This is the only thing you will be. But something has been added to that "you," and that is what you are trying to get rid of. That is what longing is. That is what meditation is. It is to recognize that you are obsessed with disturbance and you need to turn towards the stillness. You are obsessed with that white spot, but that is not what you are searching for. You are searching for the darkness that is surrounding it.

If someone tells you there's a bigger white spot with more luxuries, more comfort, and you will go there after you die, look at them and just laugh. "I am trying to get rid of this white spot so that I can become the darkness - I can become the very space I'm in. Now you are pointing me to another white spot that is somewhere else. And you're filling my mind with more imagination - that this is not the white spot that I should be looking for."

The real understanding happens in love. And that starts by fully accepting, understanding, and acknowledging that you have no idea what you're searching for. You cannot create a mental construct of what you're searching for. You are ignorant. That is why you need to search.

A learned man approached Nazruddin and asked, "Mullah, can you teach me everything you know in one session?" Nazruddin replied, "Of course, but it'll cost you." The man agreed to pay and asked Nazruddin to begin. Nazruddin simply said, "I have taught you everything I know." And collected his payment.

At least he knows that he does not know anything. Acceptance of ignorance is the beginning of the search. Show me the one who can say, "I don't know." I'll show you a Buddha. Just show me the one who can fully accept, deep down, without any doubt that he knows nothing. Everything he knows about the world, everything he thinks he knows about the world, is all part of the same ignorance.

The greatest of scientific theories, the greatest of religious expositions, the deepest of philosophical understandings - if he can look at the totality of everything that is given to him, that is not a part of his knowledge. This is all borrowed. He was born into this world with all this information already existing. He did not earn the right to understand any of it. He just read a book, heard a conversation, or he sat in a classroom, and this information was dumped on him whether he wanted it or not. There was no longing to know any of this. It just happened, depending on what kind of religious background you were born into, depending on what kind of school you went to, depending on what kind of books you were reading. Accidentally, you picked up some murmurings in the forest, and you started inquiring more and more about the rustling of leaves, the movement of trees. "What is this?" And then you created a concept out of it, an idea out of it, and that is what you call your life. And now when you walk into life, when you look at nature, when you look at the experiences outside, you don't look at it with a sense of wonder. You look at it with arrogance. "I know what clouds are. I know what lightning is. I know what the sun is. I know what water is - it's two molecules of hydrogen, one molecule of oxygen. And the sun also contains hydrogen." It's all concepts and theories. How can you search for the truth? How can you search for yourself if you're stuck in the world of imagination, if you're refusing to even accept that you don't know anything - if you have substituted theoretical ideas for experiential knowledge, and if you call that your intelligence.

"I'm a science major. All this spiritual stuff, it sounds so silly. Sitting quiet. I've studied for years. I've acquired my PhD. I know so much." Your PhD is what is blocking your true self, what is separating you from your true self. And there's not a single individual who doesn't think that he has not acquired some kind of PhD in some domain of his life. Each individual believes that he knows something. That "knowing" is the false knowing. That knowing is the shadow that is blocking the light. That knowing which has no basis in existence, it is just in your mind. It is just in the world of your imagination.

It's just like the letter "a". Where is the letter "a"? You and a few other human beings know about it because it's a purely imaginary symbol that was created to designate something, like "a" is for apple. Apple doesn't know that "a" is for apple. But for you, that "a" is very important - so important that if you were to remove "a" from your life, your whole world would collapse. Imagine - you cannot form a single sentence, a single coherent sentence without it. You cannot tell the story of your life. You cannot do science. You cannot do mathematics. You cannot do religion. Just one single letter, drop it.

In fact, that is what spirituality is all about. You don't have to drop everything - just drop one thing. Just drop the letter "a". Live as if the letter "a" does not exist. That is when you will see what the problem is in dropping. It's because you have built your whole world on lies. You built your whole empire on deception. Your whole kingdom is built on sandy soil. It's not on firm ground. Just the very thought of shifting a few sand grains shakes your whole being. And that is why you say, "This lie is better because I have spent so much time here. I have invested too much in this. I don't want to know the truth."

It's not because the truth is far away. It's not because it's difficult to search for it. It's not because you have to be something special to find it. No. It's because of what you have done. When you were not searching for the truth, you did not simply sit quiet. When you were not searching for the truth, you were not idle. You were building on the lies. And now you've built a whole world out of a simple idea that you are searching for yourself. That is why dropping is hard. And the dropping cannot happen without accepting that you know nothing.

That's the starting point of a spiritual quest. The moment you are able to say, "I know nothing," you have already arrived. From there, it is only a matter of time before you become the truth, before the truth fills you. Can you do that? Because a teacher cannot do that for you - your friends cannot do that for you. Society, the world cannot do that for you. Only you can say, "I don't know." Because if somebody else says you don't know, it hurts your ego. In a way, they are saying that they know something that you don't. But when you say it, there is no ego involved. You don't have to bring in the ego, because you are accepting ignorance at such a deep level - you're seeing the entire human race as an extension of that ignorance.

Yes. Human beings are knowledgeable in the world of shadows. They are experts in creating shadows. They're experts in describing what a shadow is, how it moves. They are masters of the shadows. But they know nothing about the light. So you can't go to someone who has made his life to talk about shadows and ask him about light. You will be disappointed. And you cannot ask yourself because you've been living in a world of shadows. Accepting that you don't know opens up the infinite possibilities - the infinite ways of finding yourself.

Don't Go Back to Sleep

The breeze at dawn has secrets to tell you.
Don't go back to sleep.
You must ask for what you really want.
Don't go back to sleep.

People are going back and forth across the doorsill
where the two worlds touch.
The door is round and open.
Don't go back to sleep.

Don't go back to sleep. Sleep is the only thing you have to overcome. And what is this sleep? Is it unconsciousness? Is it forgetfulness? Is it entering an alternate realm of reality? What is sleep? Sleep is a soul that is burdened by thoughts. Your pure spirit, when it feels heavy under the influence of thoughts, feels sleepy. And when there are enough thoughts to create enough intoxication, you are fully asleep. Sleep is intoxication - just like there are intoxicants for the body, for the mind, and the spirit.

A little bit of alcohol or a few drugs can numb your body - the body that you so dearly love, the body sensations you so fully trust, the instincts of your body that keep you alive, that keep you going. A very small thing can numb all that to a point where you can, without hesitation, fall into a ditch - your body can lose its sense of balance, sense of coordination. How easily it can happen. How much time does it take to intoxicate your body? Your body could have been vibrant, healthy, giving you all the right signals for years and years. One glass of alcohol is enough. You are intoxicated. Your body is useless.

It's the same with your spirit. You could have existed as a pure being for eons. For lifetimes, since the beginning of time, just one thought, just one idea can intoxicate it. It can take away all the vibrancy. It can take away all the true nature, the way it moves, the way it lives. All that can be forgotten - the true aliveness, the true wakefulness - can be forgotten because a thought is an intoxicant. In fact, we are intoxicated more by thoughts than anything else. We can live without alcohol. We can live without drugs. We can live without all the physical stimulations that we are searching for, but we cannot live without mental stimulation. The way we are, we are completely, totally addicted to thoughts. It is thoughts that are our biggest addiction.

Unfortunately, there are no mental institutions where you can go to get rid of this sickness because everybody is suffering from the same sickness. Now, who will create such an institution? Who will create such a school where you can go to get rid of your thoughts? Fortunately, a few individuals have created those schools. That is what we recognize as meditation. Meditation is that school - that institution you go to with total acceptance of your ignorance, and you say, "I am sick of these thoughts. Everything I know, I know through these thoughts and I am not a thought. I am something more. I want to know the truth."

You should be totally exhausted with your life. You should be frustrated with your searching. You should be squirming in pain that you have lived in a world of imaginary thoughts. There should be a deep anguish, then you can go to meditation. You can go to a teacher - not a teacher who can add more things to you, but can take away your thoughts. Take away that burden.

What is weighing you down? Your soul is free. It has always been free. The sky is vast enough, the wings are wide enough, and the breeze is just perfect to keep you afloat, to keep you flying for as long as you want - nothing more is needed. All the ingredients are there. Existence is reminding you that you have it in you, you can fly, but something is weighing you down. You're tied to something. Your wings are tied to something. Every time you try to fly, you fall to the ground. And what is that? The burden of thoughts. The heaviest thing in human experience is a thought. All other things are light when compared to a thought.

Nazruddin was seen struggling to carry a heavy load of firewood on his back. A passerby stopped and said, "Mullah, why don't you put that load down? It looks heavy." Nazruddin replied, "Oh, no. I can't do that. This load is much easier to carry than the thought of carrying it."

We are burdened by thoughts, and that is what is our drowsiness. That is our sleep. There is nothing else stopping us from experiencing our true nature. There's nothing blocking the way. The gate is wide open, there's nobody pushing and shoving, and there's no queue. It's waiting there. It's inviting you. It's telling you to come. But you are unable to move because you don't want to go alone. You want to carry all your thoughts. You want to take the idea of who you are. You want to take your body. You want to take your mind. You want to take your children. You want to take your friends, your relatives. You want to save the whole world. You want to save the dolphins, but you're not willing to save yourself.

You can only go naked. You cannot carry any of these things. And what is the definition of naked? Without any thoughts. Naked in spirituality - it's not taking off your clothes. That's the easiest thing to do. But can you take off the clothing of your thoughts? Can you take off the idea? Even if you take off your clothes, you can still be holding on to the idea. Every moment you are thinking - when you are naked, you're actually thinking about clothes. Look at the nature of the mind. You've thrown the clothes away, but you're carrying them with you. You want to go beyond your material needs. You want to rise above the animal level. You want to go beyond all your basic instincts, but you're carrying all of them with you. That is the burden.

So you have to find that mental institution, that unique mental institution, that is dedicated to introducing the sickness - that is dedicated to showing you that you're sick. That's what meditation is. Meditation is that institution where you're not allowed to do anything else. Once you go into that institution, they'll tell you to sit in one place and watch your sickness. That's it. That's the method. That's the pill. That's the electric treatment. That's all the treatments. Sit and watch your sickness. Sooner or later, you realize that, yes, there is sickness, and you will also realize that you can easily step away from it. Just the realization that you are not the sickness because you can watch it, is enough to drop it. But this has to happen experientially. That is why it takes a little time. It won't happen instantaneously. You just have to trust the process and sit and watch the disturbance, watch the sickness. Sooner or later, you will be separated.

Stay together, friends.
Don't scatter and sleep.
Our friendship is made
of being awake.

That's our true nature. We can only meet in wakefulness. Otherwise, we are strangers to each other. We will always be strangers. You might know a little bit about me. You might know something about the way I look or the way I speak. You might know a little bit about my thoughts, but you will not know who I am.

We can meet. We are friends on the journey of awakening. We are here to talk about our destination. We are here to share our experiences. We are here to help each other reach there. But ultimately, what we are looking for, is that deep communion with ourselves so that we both can look into each other and meet for the first time.

And when can we meet? We can meet only when we have gone beyond sleep. We both are longing to meet each other, but we are stuck in a dream. And we are trying to wake ourselves up. We are using words. We are using experiences. We are making as much noise as possible. We are searching in as many different ways as possible, but our meeting is not possible as long as we are in this dream.

Wakefulness is where we meet. Don't fall asleep. Fight the sleep. That's your last struggle. Sleep is your ultimate obstacle. If you are able to go beyond sleep, we can meet because that is when the meeting is perfect. That is when love is perfect because there is no other. That is when we realize there was never another. We both were two images reflecting on the same mirror. Both of us belong to the same mirror. We were only separated in our minds.

But whether you want it or not, eventually, you have to come back to your original nature. You can fall asleep again and again. You can start searching for yourself on the outside, you can be lost in that searching. You can ask for many things. You can have hundreds and thousands of wishes. "I want this. I want that." But, eventually, only one wish will be granted because existence can listen to only one wish - your wish to become yourself. All other wishes will be denied.

Three men were stranded on a deserted island when they discovered a magical goldfish tangled in a fishing net near the shore. The goldfish, grateful for being freed from the net, offers each of them one wish. The first man excitedly says, "I wish to be rich." In an instant, he finds himself surrounded by piles of gold coins and valuable treasures. The second man, not wanting to be outdone, declares "I wish to be reunited with my family." Suddenly, he's transported back home, embracing his loved ones with tears of joy. Finally, it's the third man's turn. He ponders for a moment and then says, "You know, I'm feeling quite lonely without my friends. I wish they were back here with me." Just like that, the first two men reappeared on the island.

The only wish that you can actually ask for, that cannot be taken away from you once it's granted, is the wish to become yourself, is the wish to know yourself. All other things you can ask for, existence only appears to be giving it to you - you will only be given those things momentarily. Eventually, even if you were to be given all that you want, you cannot be given the wish to be eternally alive. There is death lurking in the corner. How can you go beyond that? Without understanding death, all your other wishes are useless because finally, death will come and say, "Bring all those idiots back. I have come."

Find yourself before death comes and says, "Now it does not matter. Only my wish will be fulfilled." Eventually, death will win. Your wish cannot compete against the wishes of death. Death is ultimate. So before that happens, find yourself. Because what can death do to the one who has become himself? There is nothing to take away from him. There's no body to take away. There's no mind to take away. There are no desires to take away. What the hell will death do with the one who's awakened? It'll come and it'll say "Hi", and it'll go away. It has no job. That much is your possibility. You can transcend even death.

But it all starts with knowing that you don't know anything. And you cannot find what you're looking for. You are searching for your lover. But you are that lover. You will not find yourself. You can only become yourself.

ENTERTAIN THEM ALL

Welcome and entertain them all.

Even if they are a crowd of sorrows,
who violently sweep your house, empty of its
furniture.

Still, treat each guest honorably.

He may be clearing you out for some new delight.

There's a state of mind which accepts everything that
is happening inside and outside with the least
disturbance. The condition is inbuilt in the mind as
much as the mind is the seat of chaos and
disturbance. There is a way to understand the mind
which can help us bring it to a state where it is
perceiving things with the same intensity,
understanding things using the same intelligence,
being judgmental, and being useful, with one
difference - it is not disturbing. That is the state of
mind we are actually striving for.

Our effort is not to fully empty the mind because we
don't know what that really means. It is just an idea

because everything you know, you know it through your mind. It's like saying, "Live without a head, exist without the brain, exist without thinking." There's no way for you to understand what that state is. In fact, only at the moment of awakening, only in an enlightened state, the ultimate state of transcendence of the mind and the body, in that experience of Samadhi, you are beyond thoughts, you are beyond your mind - you are beyond the continuous thinking process. Otherwise, even during moments of deep meditation, moments of deep relaxation, even when you are experiencing a sense of bliss and joy in meditation, you are not beyond the mind. You are only beyond the disturbance of the mind.

Now, where is the mind? What is the mind doing? How has it lost its ability to disturb you? By its very nature, disturbance happens because we interact with our thoughts. We are watching our thoughts. We are seeing something that is happening on the screen of our mind. And sometimes, it excites us, sometimes it puts us into action, and sometimes it disturbs us.

The same thing is happening when you're sitting in deep meditation. In a state of mental calmness, you are experiencing the same thoughts. But somehow, the mind has lost its ability to sting. It has lost its sticky nature. It is flowing like a smooth river. The noise and chaos of the mind have become the music of the stream. The same noise, same chaos is registering on your being as gentle vibrations. What has changed?

There are two things that change when you go deeper into meditation. One is the distance between your point of awareness and your point of perception. It expands in meditation. Without meditation, it is difficult to maintain a distance between your point of awareness and the mind itself. In fact, you are sucked right into the middle of the activities of the mind.

In deeper states of meditation, there is a perceptible, recognizable space between your point of awareness and your thoughts. Now, that space reduces the noise and intensity of your thoughts. It creates a buffer zone, a gap where you can simply observe the thoughts without being entangled in them. You watch the thoughts come and go like passing clouds in the sky.

The second thing that changes in meditation is the quality of awareness itself. In normal waking consciousness, awareness is bound by the limitations of the ego, the constant identification with thoughts and emotions. But as you meditate, your awareness starts to expand and become more expansive, like the sky that holds everything without being disturbed.

As you go deeper into meditation, you realize that thoughts are just passing phenomena, and you are the witness of these phenomena. The identification with thoughts weakens, and you experience a deeper sense of inner stillness and peace. With regular practice, this expanded awareness and the gap between your point of awareness and perception become more stable. The mind gradually loses its grip on you, and you become less reactive to its fluctuations.

This state of mental calmness and equanimity is not a suppression of thoughts or an escape from them. It is a transcendence of the mind's limitations and a recognition of your true nature beyond the constant mental chatter. In this state, you experience the mind as a tool that you can use when needed, but you are no longer a slave to its every whim. You become the master of your mind, and it no longer disturbs you as it once did.

Meditation is the key to unlocking this inner peace and freedom from the mind's turmoil. Through consistent practice and sincere effort, you can experience the profound transformation of the mind and discover the vast expanse of consciousness that lies beyond its confines.

It's natural that when something is pushed away, its impact on you reduces. You're listening to the same thing. You're going through the same experiences. But the whole experience has mellowed down. It has softened. That is the first thing that happens.

The second thing that happens is the noise is reduced because the space is increased. Along with this, there's also a deep acceptance of what's happening in your mind, because you can still continue to fight with your thoughts. Even when you're listening to the thoughts, even when you are perceiving them at a lower intensity, if you are still fully entangled in thoughts, they will still continue to disturb you. Even a whisper of something that you don't want to hear can disturb you. It need not always be a loud intense experience - even a quiet experience can shake your being.

For example, someone you know, you connect with, has died. When the news comes to you, it can either come in the form of someone screaming, yelling, writhing in pain, shouting that this person has died, or they can come quietly and say, "So-and-so has died." It doesn't matter how you hear the sound. It doesn't matter what the intensity is, your experience is the same because it is not the intensity of the connection between you and those sounds that is determining your reaction, but the connection between you and that individual. The stronger the connection, the more intense the reaction.

So as you start going deeper, the space between your point of awareness and your thoughts begins to expand. All those thoughts which are not deeply connected to your experiences of life, just pure mental noise, mechanical noise, repetitive noise - the disturbance of all that naturally settles down, which is the majority of the mind.

And then - because you have watched your thoughts, you have understood how they are impacting you, you have spent enough time observing the thoughts, you have learned to accept them just the way they are - you have stopped fighting with your thoughts. This ability to be with the mind, listen to the mind, experience the mind, and still not get disturbed by it is only possible when you know this state of deep acceptance.

It is not enough to just distance yourself from the mind. It is not enough to distance yourself from the scene of disturbance. That is why if there is a lot of chaos in and around you, you can choose to move away. You can go to a quieter place. Yes, the disturbance reduces, but only one form of disturbance reduces - the disturbance that is coming from things that you really don't want to hear.

Let's say, suddenly, you find yourself in the middle of a busy marketplace. You were just taking a walk, intending to enjoy the sounds of nature. However, you unintentionally entered a busy marketplace, and the disturbance there has nothing personal to do with you. It is just pure noise and chaos. This type of external disturbance is relatively easy to deal with - all you have to do is move away from the busy area.

But, if something is troubling you inside your realm of thoughts, if there are unresolved emotions or past traumas, if you have many experiences that you struggle with daily, it becomes impossible to reduce that disturbance by simply running away physically. In fact, you can try to escape by going as far as possible, hoping to leave your problems behind, but you will still be carrying them within you. The internal disturbance will persist unless you address and reconcile with it directly.

One day, Nazruddin was seen running frantically through the streets. A passerby stopped him and asked, "Nazruddin, why are you running so fast?" Nazruddin replied, "I am running away from my problems." The passerby, puzzled, asked, "But can you really run away from your problems?" Nazruddin, still running, replied, "No, but I can run faster than my problems can catch me."

That is what we often tend to do - running away from our problems, trying to distance ourselves from them. However, there is no way to distance ourselves from a problem without fully understanding it. What if the problem lies within the mind itself? What if it is the very nature of the mind, its movement, and the conditioning that affect us? If that is the case, then the only way to go beyond our problems is to completely transcend the mind. But the mind will not let us go beyond it without us fully comprehending it.

Now, what is the mind? It is a pattern, a rhythm, and repetition. Once the mind identifies certain things that are causing disturbance, it holds on to them, repeatedly presenting them until we address and resolve those issues. Once we genuinely resolve them, the intensity of those thoughts reduces, and eventually, they subside. Thus, understanding the mind is essential to move beyond it. With understanding comes acceptance, and with acceptance comes a sense of settling down. As Rumi wisely says, **"Welcome and entertain them all, even if they are a crowd of sorrows."** We should treat all experiences with equanimity.

To achieve this, we need to be rooted in the experience of the present moment. If we are lost in our thoughts, being chased by them, or engulfed in them, it becomes challenging to perceive pain and pleasure with equanimity. We may experience moments of pleasure with deep intensity, unconscious of the fact that pleasure is inherently connected to pain. Consequently, we become completely absorbed in pleasure, only to experience an equal intensity of pain when the mind shifts its focus. This happens because we become entangled with our thoughts and emotions.

You can be an entire ocean, but sometimes you can become so attached to a single wave that your identity becomes fully intertwined with that one wave. This is why one problem - if an individual perceives it to be significant enough, deep enough, and insurmountable, - can ruin their life. They may even consider ending their life solely because they are unable to solve this one problem. What does this signify? It means they have forgotten that they are the ocean and have become identified with just one wave.

But how can you forget the vastness of the ocean - the very ocean through which you breathe, walk, and live. So many other things are happening that have nothing to do with your incessant thinking. Yet, you can get so lost in your thoughts that you forget about everything else. This is the nature of attachment. When attachment to thoughts occurs, it becomes absolute. As a result, when there is pleasure, you become the pleasure, and when there is pain, you become the pain. Since you don't want to be the pain, you try to push those experiences away. However, this is not the meditative or Sufi way.

The Sufi way is to cultivate mindfulness, beingness, and presence even when there is nothing to do, no problems to solve, no relaxation to seek, and no desire to improve oneself. The Sufi is constantly working on the art of being, always remembering themselves. "Zikr," the remembrance of the divine, is essentially the remembrance of one's own being. The more you remember yourself, the more rooted you become in the present moment. This rootedness eventually allows you to perceive things with equanimity.

Welcome and entertain them all!
Even if they are a crowd of sorrows,
who violently sweep your house
empty of its furniture,

Still, treat each guest honorably.
He may be clearing you out
for some new delight.

How can you be certain that the chaos, confusion, and disturbance you are experiencing are not clearing out unwanted things to make room for peace, joy, and happiness? How do you know? You are categorizing your experiences based on your limited perspectives and not seeing your life in its totality. Lost in thoughts, you have learned to label and categorize thoughts as useful, useless, positive, or negative without realizing their fluid and changing nature. Sometimes, what may appear as a useful thought can seem useless, and disturbance and chaos can actually lead to clarity and peace.

Due to this limited perspective, it is better not to choose and categorize thoughts. This might be a difficult concept to grasp for someone who is deeply immersed in the mind and believes that life revolves around watching, categorizing, and favoring positive thoughts while pushing away negative ones. For those who are lost in the mind, this seems to be the only way to live, resulting in a chaotic way of living.

Looking at everything with equanimity might appear foreign to those lost in the mind. However, this itself should be a sign that being lost in the mind leads to a chaotic existence. Embracing a more open, non-judgmental perspective allows you to see beyond the noise of the mind and gain a deeper understanding of life. In this way, you can experience greater peace and harmony within yourself and with the world around you.

There is no way to escape the disturbance of the mind as long as you are stuck in the mind. Rumi talks about a higher way of living, a different approach to experiences. Up until now, you have divided your experiences, and your entire effort has been towards keeping these thoughts divided. This arrangement is recognized as your social structure, your religious structure, your understanding of life, your knowledge, and your wisdom - all used to divide your experiences. However, if there was no necessity to divide, if you were to accept all your experiences with equanimity, and if there is a way to experience everything equally and yet not be disturbed, then all the basic structures you have created for yourself, concepts, and ideas will fall apart.

Take, for example, the idea of heaven and hell. Why is there a necessity to divide experiences into heavenly and hellish ones? Heaven and hell are not physical places; they are experiences that you like or dislike. This divide is the very essence of religions. But what if you could say, "I don't mind. I will not choose this or that in my internal world?" Of course, in the external world, it's a different matter. If there is a ditch and a safe path, instinctively, you choose the safe path. Your body has an in-built survival mechanism, and your mind understands that.

Even after you become enlightened and transcend the mind, if you encounter a dangerous situation, like seeing a snake while taking a walk, you will instinctively react to protect yourself. That instinct is a fundamental force that keeps you alive, a basic law of existence. While you can choose equanimity in your internal world, your body's survival instincts still play a crucial role in the external world. The journey of awakening is about understanding this delicate balance and finding freedom and peace amidst the dynamic interplay of the internal and external experiences.

That is why it does not matter whether you're enlightened or not. If you're climbing up the ladder, for whatever reason, and you slip, immediately, you'll grab hold of the ladder. It doesn't matter who you are; your reaction is always the same because these things are not consciously done - they are all inbuilt. Equanimity has nothing to do with the external world. It's all about inside because that is where disturbance is, that is where chaos is. In the internal world, you're constantly dividing your experiences - "I like this person, I don't like this person. I like this community, I don't like that community. I don't want to be poor, I want to be rich. I don't want to be lonely, I want to have lots of friends." That is what you call your life - dividing your experiences. However, there is a higher way of living, and that is to accept all experiences as a part of your being. They all have an important role to play.

What you're experiencing as pain now might actually be healing. If not for that pain, you would have probably exploded. For all you know, something has already acknowledged your deeper suffering, and it has been treating it. The wound is clearing out; the wound is healing, and that is what you're observing as pain. Sometimes, very deep emotional and psychological pain is hidden by the mind, pushed into the subconscious. So, when you are actually able to see pain, it is an indication that a deeper pain has lessened to a point where now the mind thinks, "I can show this to him. He's not going to freak out. He's not going to jump off a building." The mind, too, has a survival mechanism, just like the body.

The mind can be whimsical and chaotic, pushing you into action all the time. But if you're standing at the edge of a cliff, tell your mind to push you off, and see what it does. All it takes is a single thought, and it can easily make you jump off the cliff. However, it doesn't do that because it knows that if you die, it dies. It has a deep attachment to the body at a certain level because its identity is intermixed with the body. The mind is connected to your pure self, which is transcendental, but on this end, it is connected to the body and always sees itself as a part of the body. The mind's journey is to realize its true nature, free from the limitations of the body and the incessant mental chatter.

The survival mechanism of the body applies to the mind as well, so it won't push you off the cliff. Look at the movement of the mind and how it communicates things to you without your permission, accessing all the information, including your deepest pain and suffering. Without this choice it makes on its own, deciding what to show and what not to show, it could easily drive you insane. Some of your deepest pains are not even visible to you. They may manifest in your dreams or be triggered accidentally. Your mind creates support structures to help you deal with these hidden aspects.

Life is not as simple as identifying with every emotion that arises. You can experience a range of emotions like anger, frustration, sadness, and joy without fully attaching yourself to them. All emotions are allowed, but when you forget yourself and build your identity solely on them, you can easily get lost in a state of disturbance.

The mind's repetitive nature can contribute to this disturbance. If it were to introduce a problem once, gain your attention, and then move on, the nature of thinking would be different. But the mind tends to bring back the same problem again and again, leading to unnecessary worry and mental turmoil. Understanding the nature of the mind and its repetitive patterns is essential in finding a way to go beyond its disturbances.

Imagine you're the president, and an important file is brought to you for signing. You look at it, sign it, and once it's done, the file is gone, not to return. However, your mind operates differently. It brings back the same file, showing it to you again and again, even though you've already read and signed it. The mind seems insistent on making you read it once more. It wants to ensure that you truly understand the problem, not just acknowledge it. The mind doesn't care about mere acknowledgment; it seeks genuine understanding. And this understanding goes beyond the intellectual level. If you merely grasp something intellectually, the mind won't remove it from circulation.

To the mind, understanding means that you have seen the issue so profoundly that you no longer need to pay it any attention. You let it pass by without getting caught up in its repetitive nature. Only then will the mind let go of the issue and eventually let it disappear. It craves a level of comprehension that goes beyond surface-level acknowledgment, something that touches the core of your being. When the mind observes that you've reached this depth of understanding, it will finally allow the issue to dissolve, no longer bringing it back repeatedly.

Ultimately, the key lies in developing a profound understanding of the mind's repetitive patterns and finding a way to transcend them. With this level of understanding, you can avoid being entangled in the same problems repeatedly and experience a sense of freedom and peace within.

Meditation is a dedicated effort and practice because the mind keeps bringing back the same files again and again. Without observing them impartially and without attachment, the mind will persist in its repetition. It takes time to sink deeper into your being and reach a point of deeper settling and understanding. Once that happens, the mind recognizes that there's no need to present those thoughts on the screen of your mind anymore.

When you've observed something repeatedly without attachment, the mind subconsciously knows that you won't engage with it even if it comes up again. Your awareness has shifted inward, and you're no longer caught up in the same thought patterns. This process is referred to as 'going in' or 'going deeper.'

For the first time, you start leaving your experiences without judgment. You let the mind continue its repetitions without your interference. This practice is necessary to break the cycle of the mind's persistent and repetitive nature. It is essential to become a witness to these thoughts without getting entangled in them.

In meditation, you begin to experience this shift, and as you continue to practice, you strengthen your ability to stay present, centered, and detached from the mind's repetitive patterns. This leads to greater clarity, inner peace, and the ability to live more authentically and joyfully in the present moment.

A duck walks into a convenience store and asks the clerk, "Do you have any grapes?" The clerk looks at the duck strangely and says, "No, sorry, we don't sell grapes here." The next day the duck comes into the store and asks the clerk, "Do you have any grapes?" The annoyed clerk replied, "No. I told you yesterday, we don't sell grapes here." The third day, the duck comes back into the store and asks the same question again. "Do you have any grapes?" The clerk, now very angry, says, "Look, I told you already, we don't have any grapes. And if you come back in here asking for grapes again, I'm going to nail your beak to the floor." The next day, the duck comes back into the store, and asks the clerk, "Do you have any nails?" The clerk replies, "No. We don't have any nails." The duck then says, "Do you have any grapes?"

That's precisely how the mind operates. It is persistent and relentless, which is why it holds such a strong grip over us. The mind doesn't have an ego, so it doesn't give up easily. It can keep presenting the same thoughts and patterns repeatedly until we fully grasp and transcend them. Even at times when it seems to deviate or take us away from certain thoughts, it ultimately brings us right back to them.

The Whirling Dervish

I AM NOT FROM THIS WORLD

Not Christian or Jew or Muslim,
not Hindu, Buddhist, Sufi, or Zen.

Not any religion or cultural system.
I am not from the east or the west,

Not out of the ocean or up from the ground,
Not natural or ethereal, not composed of elements at
all.

I do not exist, am not an entity in this world or the
next,
Did not descend from Adam and Eve or any origin
story.

My place is placeless, a trace of the traceless.
Neither body or soul.

You are something totally different than what you
think you are, and you have the right to know who
you truly are. The entire quest for understanding
yourself, for deepening your self-awareness, arises
from the realization that your current perception of
yourself is limited and restrictive. The life you lead
based on this limited understanding can never bring
you true satisfaction.

You are vast, expansive, and limitless in your essence. Even if you were to achieve everything that every person on this planet desires, and all those desires were to be fulfilled, you would still feel incomplete. This is because you perceive yourself as a mere cup when, in reality, you are the entire ocean.

Just like you, other people move around with their cups and have their unique desires. However, if you were to recognize that you are the entire ocean, able to hold every desire of every individual, you would still feel unfulfilled if you don't realize the fundamental nature of your being. Your body is just a cup submerged in the ocean, and it's crucial to understand that you are not the cup but the vast and boundless ocean itself.

It is impossible to fill limitations. By their very nature, limitations will always remain as such, no matter how much effort is exerted to fill or complete them. Your desires, in a way, represent the effort you put in to try and overcome this sense of incompleteness. However, no one can claim that the accomplishment of their desires has brought them true completion. Despite the countless individuals from different backgrounds and pursuits - kings, queens, politicians, religious figures, scientists, artists, and many others - engaging in various searches and pursuits, there is not a single example in the outer world where an individual has truly found fulfillment solely through their desiring process.

This fact should lead us to realize that there is something fundamentally flawed in our search for fulfillment in the external world. We seem to be forgetting the most crucial thing - the search for our true selves. Amidst our busyness in trying to utilize our minds and bodies to achieve limited objectives in the world, we have forgotten that there is a path to use our minds and bodies to reach the boundless.

Rumi, in his profound wisdom, asserts, "**I don't belong to this world. Not a Christian or Jew or Muslim, not Hindu, Buddhist, or Zen. Not any religion or cultural system.**" He emphasizes that he does not associate himself with any specific class, division, or sect because all these are limitations imposed on the human body, which is already a limitation in itself. Religions exist to explain something about our bodies, not about our true selves. This is precisely why their concepts are flawed, as they do not apply to the real essence of who we are.

Rumi is breaking free from all the shackles of categorization. Some people perceive themselves purely from a materialistic standpoint, viewing themselves as nothing more than their physical bodies. On the other hand, there are those who identify as spiritual beings, believing themselves to be the soul or the spirit. However, Rumi proclaims, "I am neither." He speaks the truth, highlighting that the true nature of being cannot be confined to any categorization. All such categorizations are bound by the limitations of our experiences and our senses.

You are something transcendent and pure, far beyond any label or classification. To truly know and understand this aspect of yourself, you must become one with it. Embracing the oneness of your being is the key to realizing your boundless and profound nature.

ABOUT AVI

Born and raised in India, Avi's professional journey in the corporate world began soon after he graduated from college. However, at the age of 24, he recognized an emptiness within that material success could never satisfy. Yearning for inner tranquility and a sense of purpose, he made the courageous decision to move away from home, leave his job, and embark on a dedicated pursuit of meditation.

Devoting himself to intense meditation for three years, Avi underwent a profound spiritual awakening that forever transformed his life. Driven by this newfound realization, he eagerly began sharing his experience through various programs and retreats. In 2017, he traveled to America and intuitively knew that he had found a place to sow the seeds of consciousness and awareness.

Currently, Avi resides and teaches in Tennessee, where the first Nirvana meditation center is being developed. He speaks twice a day, and his talks are recorded and transcribed by his students, which are ultimately compiled into books for publication.

Nirvana Foundation is a nonprofit spiritual community providing individuals with an opportunity to explore the realms of meditation and self-awareness through books and programs.

Visit www.nirvana.foundation to learn more about Avi and his vision.

BOOKS BY AVI

 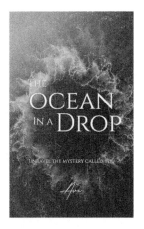

ISBN: 979-8374196740   ISBN: 979-8852311207

 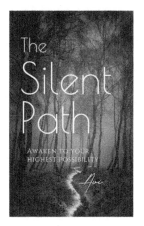

ISBN: 979-8392250196   ISBN: 978-0578637068

ISBN: 978-1962685023

Printed in Great Britain
by Amazon